THEY LAUGHED WHEN I WROTE ANOTHER BOOK ABOUT PRAYER...

THEN THEY READ IT

How To Make Prayer Work

Dr. Gil Stieglitz

Copyright © Gil Stieglitz 2011

ISBN: 978-0-9831958-3-2
Christian Living/Theology

Published by Thriving Churches Int'l, Inc., Minden, NV 89423
www.thrivingchurches.com

Cover Design by John Chase

All Rights Reserved

All Scripture verses are from the New American Standard Bible unless otherwise indicated. New American Standard Bible: 1995 update. 1995 La Habra, CA: The Lockman Foundation.

Dedication

This book is dedicated to **God the Father, God the Son, and God the Holy Spirit** who faithfully meet with me in prayer through Biblical Meditation each day.

1 John 1:3

Table of Contents

Introduction: The Foundation of Prayer 7
Biblical Meditation 10
How to Get Started Praying in this New Way: Great Verses 23
Slow Repetition of the Bible 28
Memorization of the Bible 36
Study of the Bible 44
Singing the Bible 49
Confessing the Bible 55
Praying the Bible 67
Envisioning the Bible 73
Personalizing the Bible 114
Journaling Your Interactions With the Bible 121
Diagram or Analogize the Bible 126
Personal Translation of the Bible 130
Further Exercises in Biblical Meditation 134
Conclusion: Rockets have just been strapped to your life 138

Appendices

Appendix #1 Bible Study 152
Appendix #2 Biblical Meditation 163
Appendix #3 Blank Worksheets 171
Appendix #4 How to use this book 174

INTRODUCTION: THE FOUNDATION OF PRAYER

Jesus said,
"If you abide in Me, and My words abide in you, ask whatever you wish, and it will be done for you."
John 15:7

I want to change the way you pray and the way you think about prayer. Many of us think of prayer as boring, ineffective, and hardly life transforming. But the truths in this book make prayer transformative, liberating, powerful, and even enticing. I want to show you something so foundational and so dynamic about prayer that if you do it, your life will never recover. I want to show you the secrets to prayer that make it work. Is there a way of thinking and acting in my spirituality that makes prayer exciting, transforming, and powerful? The answer is yes.

For well over a thousand year Christians had a much bigger view of prayer than we in the modern world do. They thought of prayer as interacting with God, not just requesting things from Him. They knew that our requests to God were built on a foundation of life with God: listening to Him, interacting, obeying, and sharing life with Him. They knew how to fulfill Jesus' words in John 15:7 in their prayer life. "If you abide in me and my words abide in you, ask whatever you will and it will be done for you." Most Christians are aware of Jesus' words about prayer. They just don't know how to make it work. What does it mean to have His words abide in you? How do you actually pull this off every day? There is so much more to prayer than you have ever thought before. Let me give you a glimpse. Prayer is reading and studying the Scriptures. Prayer is memorizing and slowly repeating Scripture so God can speak out of His Word. Prayer is singing Scripture and personalizing it as King David did. Prayer is picturing yourself living out Scriptural commands and seeing the Bible stories take place in your head. Prayer is journaling the insights and thoughts one has about Scripture and life. All of this has been titled Biblical Meditation and not prayer and is why our prayer lives are so weak. If prayer is not built on a foundation of Scripture and abiding in Scripture, it is often weak, selfishly focused, and ineffective. It is the foundation of Scripture in your soul that gives requests their platform. Because we have divorced our requests from the Scripture we see far less results.

When I first became a Christian I was introduced to a totally different kind of prayer life that changed me dramatically. I was taught, trained, and indoctrinated into it before anyone told me it was prayer. If I had known it was prayer I probably would not have been interested in doing it. I now find myself so used to this "prayer" life that I pray for one to three hours every day. I am learning and loving the interaction with God and the life change it brings. I was told that serious Christians repeated the words and phrases of the Bible as they went to sleep and at various parts of the day. This was called Biblical Meditation. I hesitate to call it prayer, lest you be discouraged to put these secrets into practice. But these methods are the secrets to praying and seeing results. Biblical Meditation forms the forgotten secrets to effective prayer. Biblical Meditation forms the foundation for all other kinds of prayer because it is the way to have God's words abiding in you.

The average Christian does not know how to pray for longer than five minutes; this is usually because their prayers are based upon a self-focused platform. They come into the presence of the most amazing and dynamic personage in the whole of our universe and eternity and they can only think to talk about themselves and what they want. Almost all Christians want to have prayer work for them, but they do not know how. Most have tried to pray and are frustrated with what little happens when they pray. Many give up and figure that prayer is only for super spiritual people but not for them. This book is designed to teach and train you in the secrets that will change the way you pray and your whole attitude to prayer. If you do these then it will change your whole life also. The Scriptures guarantee it.

This book is designed to teach you to enter the powerful world of Biblical Meditation. Biblical Meditation is a form of prayer and the foundation for prayer. It allows you to experience God speaking back to you through the Scriptures. Biblical Meditation forms your prayers from His clear desires for you instead of your own self-focused ideas. When your prayers are based and bathed in Scripture then they are transformative and radically powerful. There are a large number of verses that describe significant blessings that will come to the believer who meditates upon the Bible. There are also significant verses that promise that prayers based upon the Bible will have God's attention and answer. Biblical Meditation is the way to put this all together.

BIBLICAL MEDITATION
The Secrets to Making Prayer Work

A month before I turned seventeen, right at the time I became a Christian, two men challenged me to begin meditating on the Bible as I went to bed at night. They pushed me to begin slowly repeating a verse of Scripture as I was lying in bed waiting to fall asleep. So I tried it. I choose Psalm 1:1-3 as the verses. I began slowly saying Psalm 1:1-3 as I lay there waiting for sleep to come. This simple prayer practice strapped rockets to my life, and I am still gaining altitude.

Psalm 1:1-3
How blessed is the man who does not walk
in the counsel of the ungodly
Nor stand in the path of sinners
Nor sit in the seat of the scornful
But his delight is in the law of the Lord
And in His law he meditates day and night
And he will be like a tree firmly planted
by streams of water
Which yields its fruit in its season,
its leaf doesn't wither
And in whatever he does he prospers.

I started saying the words to the above Psalm slowly, thinking about what they meant and what I should do to live them out. I also listened to what God would speak in my soul about those words. I ended up saying those words a dozen to two dozen times at least every night before sleep would come. Because of this Scripture I thought about who I should stop listening to. The actual faces of the ungodly adults and teens began flashing into my mind. I thought about the different lifestyles that crossed my life and the results of those ways of living. The faces and lifestyle choices of alcoholic neighbors, drug addicted kids, party girls, liars, and popular kids who got away with murder started popping into my mind. I thought about my reputation as the king of the put-downs and how it didn't fit the positive instructions of this verse. I thought of two girls in particular who I had deeply wounded through arrogance and sarcastic put downs. I realized I would have to apologize or the destruction of this verse would become true of me.

After running these verses through my mind over and over, I thought about the Ten Commandments and the stories in the first five books of Moses. If I was going to be blessed like David, I was going to have to become much more familiar with the stories of the Bible. Much later I realized that I was living the life of Cain not Abel, impulsively acting upon whatever impulse came into my head. I just kept saying the words of this Psalm slowly over and over, allowing my mind to ask questions and seek answers. This Psalm became like a portable GPS guidance device guiding my life in God's way. God taught me to avoid bad people. He taught me to find righteous truth and act on it. This three-verse section became for three months the answer to almost every question in my life. All because I said it a few dozen times every night.

I said these three verses of Psalm 1 every night for over three months as I went to sleep. I put this Psalm to music and sang it some nights. I drew pictures and schematics of what this particular section of Psalms was saying. I started journaling the new ideas and insights that I was receiving about this Psalm and life in general. I confessed my sin any time I sensed God telling me I violated the truths in this Psalm. I personalized this Psalm putting my name into it every place I could. I said it over and over again. I even began carrying my journal with me during the day so I could write down insights and ideas that God brought to my mind. I found myself saying this Psalm slowly throughout the day.

I never thought of this as prayer. It was Biblical Meditation, and I was hearing God speak to me from His word. I was changing. My thoughts became prayers even though I did not know it because I was repeating Scripture over and over. God was paying attention to my thoughts, my actions, and my changes because they were prompted from the Scriptures

It was right after I started doing this that the changes started. Instead of dreading going to bed, I began to get excited to go to bed. In a few short months I started falling asleep much faster than before. I think the devil did not want me staying awake repeating Scripture. As I continued to meditate each evening on a Bible passage, my grades started to improve quickly. I developed a new ability to be able to memorize facts quickly. I was directed by God through the Scriptures to apologize to a few people who I had wronged and people started to treat me differently. Oddly, I started to run faster on the track team. I posted my best times and actually won a few races. Many of my relationships began to change for the better. I got along better with my parents; my relationship with my sister improved; I began to have more of the popular girls pay attention to me; and I developed more friends at school. I took great delight in talking and listening to God about all the stuff that was happening in my life every day. I was changing and people began noticing. A number of people asked me what was happening to me. I didn't tell them I discovered a new way of praying. I didn't even tell them I was meditating on the Bible every night. I just told people I had truly met Jesus and was having a real relationship with Him and He was changing me.

I believe the blessings that God promises for those who will meditate on the Bible began to land in my life like picnic baskets full of money. I went on to develop the habit of saying a verse or phrase from Scripture almost every night as I went to bed. I was regularly amazed at what God taught me about my just-concluded day through this simple process. There were many times when God would prepare me for the next day in specific ways through my meditation on the Scriptures the night before. Nothing that I have ever done has made as big a difference in my life as this practice of meditating on the Bible.

Since those early beginnings, I have built my life around mediating on the Scriptures in dozens of ways. I regularly use all the techniques that are listed in this book as the basis of my prayer life. It is only recently that I have realized that these practices of Biblical Meditation are really forms of prayer that allow me to experience God at a level that most Christians never enjoy. I have been puzzled at why God would answer so many of my prayers over the years and not other people I know who are fine and upright Christians. I know it is not because I am more deserving. I have come to believe that it is because the secret of transformative prayer and deep interaction with God is Biblical Meditation. We don't need new techniques to pry answers out of God; we need to spend more time learning what He has already said and live in the light of what we already know He wants. He will then go out of His way to answer prayers for that person. He wants to bless that man or woman.

As I look at my life over the last thirty-plus years, a pattern begins to emerge. When I have practiced the simple techniques of Biblical Meditation, my life has gone much better. On the other hand when I have lightened up on this practice, my life has had far less "amazing coincidences," unexpected blessings, answered prayers, and undeserved opportunities. I am a normal guy from a normal middle-class family with a secret weapon: Biblical Meditation. Through this weapon God has allowed me to receive an incredible amount of blessings and accomplish far more than I could think or imagine.

I remember just a year or so before I began praying by meditating on the Bible I was thinking of ways to make money in as lazy a way as possible. My conclusion was that welfare was probably the best way to have money and do as little as possible. But thanks to the invasion of Christ Jesus into the center of my being and the practice of slowly repeating Scripture as I went to bed, my whole life has been radically different.

Occasionally people will tell me that they look up to my prayer life and spirituality. I am amazed because I never considered this prayer. I just was taught to meditate on the Bible and listen for the voice of God in Scripture. I now realize that I was being taught to pray in the best way possible. I was trained in a secret form of prayer that opened my life up to experiencing God, receiving answers to prayer, and living a transformed life.

My life is a miracle in so many ways. Amazingly enough, I am walking proof of the climatic verse in Psalm 1:3, "And he will be like a tree firmly planted by streams of water, which yields its fruit in its season, its leaf doesn't wither, and in whatever he does he prospers." The power and blessing of God is the only reasonable explanation for my life.

God's power is real and He wants you to reach your fullest potential. With God's power you can do things that are literally impossible for you to do right now (John 14:12). Without God's power you will never reach your full potential; you may not even learn what is your full potential. Life under your own power is nothing compared to the rocket ride that can happen if you plug into God's power. The people who knew me in high school cannot believe that God could do so much with so little. I gave no evidence of being capable of the things God has done with me. God is an expert at taking the little we have and making it count so everyone knows it was Him.

In this book I will talk about all kinds of ways of praying through meditating on Scripture. But in order to unlock the power of God you don't need to do anything fancy, just start saying a verse or section of Scripture over and over again as you go to bed. You can get a new verse every night or use the same one for days and weeks.

Read and re-read a section of Scripture (Psalm 1:1-3) five times slowly and your mind will start probing, questioning, connecting, and touching the power of the living Word of God. This is prayer in a powerful form. The nutrients in a steak cannot be gained by licking the steak one time. It requires tearing, chewing, crunching, swallowing the juices, and chewing some more. In the same way the power, nutrients, and life in the Scriptures are not gained by letting your eyes glance over the page in a quick read. If you want the power that is in sacred Scripture, you will have to do more than just read.

The most transformational activity that Christians can do is to personally engage with the Bible and God directly. Every individual, every group, and every measurement confirms that a believer at any level of their growth changes the most by interacting with the Bible directly. Biblical Meditation has been clearly shown to be more transformational for the individual Christian than great worship, great preaching, serving Christ, praying, witnessing, or any other spiritual practice or church practice. This means that when people interacted with the Bible on what a particular verse might mean, how it might impact them, and what they should do that day, they are going to be changed in some way. They are going to experience the power of God in their life. The Scriptures call this Biblical Meditation. It can also be called prayer.

Listen to what the Scriptures say about the power and impact of prayerful Biblical Meditation. The power God promises for performing Biblical Meditation is staggering.

Joshua 1:8
This book of the law shall not depart from your mouth, but you shall meditate on it day and night, so that you may be careful to do according to all that is written in it; <u>for then you will make your way prosperous, and then you will have success</u>.

Notice what God says in this verse. He says if you meditate on the Bible, your life will have prosperous success. That is an amazing promise. The process of murmuring, repeating, envisioning, and studying the Scripture would guarantee success for the Ancient Israelites and for us today.

Psalm 1:1-3
*How blessed is the man who does not walk in the counsel of the wicked,
Nor stand in the path of sinners,
Nor sit in the seat of scoffers!
But his delight is in the law of the LORD,
And in His law he meditates day and night.
He will be like a tree firmly planted by streams of water,
Which yields its fruit in its season
And its leaf does not wither;
<u>And in whatever he does, he prospers.</u>*

Notice that in this series of verses that open the whole book of the Psalms, God says that one should steer clear of bad advice and instead labor to meditate on the Scriptures. God promises that if a person meditates biblically, he or she will have an amazingly fruitful and prosperous life.

Psalm 119:97-104
O how I love Your law!
It is my meditation all the day.
Your commandments make me wiser than my enemies,
For they are ever mine.
<u>I have more insight than all my teachers,</u>
For Your testimonies are my meditation.
<u>I understand more than the aged,</u>
Because I have observed Your precepts.
<u>I have restrained my feet from every evil way,</u>
That I may keep Your word.
I have not turned aside from Your ordinances,
For You Yourself have taught me.
How sweet are Your words to my taste!
Yes, sweeter than honey to my mouth!
From Your precepts I get understanding;
Therefore I hate every false way.

This is a wonderful passage ringing with the benefits that come from mediating on God's Word. The person who meditates on the Bible is wiser than their enemies. The person who meditates on the Bible is wiser than their teachers. The person who meditates on the Bible is wiser than the aged. The person who meditates on the Bible is able to keep from falling into the temptations of life. When the Bible is coursing through your soul, it provides power and a shield as well as mental virus protection.

Colossians 3:16
<u>Let the word of Christ richly dwell within you,</u> with all wisdom teaching and admonishing one another with psalms and hymns and spiritual songs, singing with thankfulness in your hearts to God.

Notice that the words of Christ need to richly dwell within the believer, not lay on the surface. The benefit of Christ's words will not do much good if they are not flowing in and through your thought-life.

2 Timothy 3:16, 17
All Scripture is inspired by God and profitable for teaching, for reproof, for correction, for training in righteousness; so that the man of God <u>may be adequate, equipped for every good work.</u>

In this verse the Bible is declared to be supernaturally inspired or breathed onto and into by God Himself. The Bible is declared to be profitable for new information, new skills, for pointing out flaws, bringing correction, and development into one's fullest potential in this life. It is the life and power of God that one gains by "chewing" and "swallowing" the words of the sacred Scriptures.

If this is the best way to bring about life change, then it is the best way to experience the power of God. If you want to transform your life in a righteous Christ-honoring direction, then you must learn how to meditate on the Bible and then you must do it every day. This means that you must set aside time for it every day. As I have said, it can start the minute that you fall asleep.

Biblical Meditation vs. Other forms of Meditation

There are three general types of meditation: Biblical, Eastern, and Materialistic. I am only advocating Biblical Meditation. Let me give you a quick overview of the three types. A very popular form of meditation in our world today is Eastern Meditation. Eastern Meditation is emptying the mind of any rational thought; to be open to the "Universe" and its "message." The idea is to say a nonsense syllable, phrase, or saying over and over again until the mind is blank. Within Eastern thought this allows you to receive cosmic messages or to be at one with the Universe. This is not what Biblical Meditation is. Christians are not trying to empty their mind to receive a subjective cosmic message, but instead Christians are trying to fill their mind with the objective message that we have already received -- the Scriptures.

A second form of meditation advocated in our modern world is Materialistic Meditation. Materialistic Meditation is filling our minds, souls, and spirits with images of all the material things that we want and desire until we unconsciously begin to chase those items. Christians are not opposed to material possessions, but we do not chase them. Christians hunger and thirst after righteousness. Christians seek first the kingdom of God and all the other things will be added to us. We do not focus our mental and spiritual energy on obtaining material possessions for our selfish use. We are interested in focusing our soul and spirit on the things of God and living the abundant life He has planned for us. We agree that focusing our mind, will, emotions, and spirit on something is powerful. We do not think that the focus of that work should be selfish, but it should be godly. We believe that one of the best things we can do for ourselves is to live for God and allow Him to fill our lives with His blessings and benefits.

The final form of meditation and the subject of this book is Biblical Meditation. Biblical Meditation shares the same name "meditation" but is really radically different with radically different purposes for its work. Biblical Meditation is filling our minds, souls, and spirits with Scripture and Scriptural concepts so that we begin living them out. In order to abide in the words of Christ and the Scriptures, you must be immersed in it. It must begin to be the way you think and reason. It must help form the pictures that you use in your head. It must be the clarifiers in your thoughts.

One is connected to power in all forms of meditation, but there are serious questions about the source of power in Eastern and Materialistic Meditation. It is only Biblical Meditation that is guaranteed to tie a person into the power of God the Father, God the Son, and God the Holy Spirit.

Eleven Forms of Biblical Meditation

There are at least eleven forms of Biblical Meditation mentioned or practiced in the Scriptures. Each form of Biblical Meditation is designed to press Scripture through your mind, will, emotions, spirit, or body so that that aspect of your being must interact with the truth of God. Too often Scripture remains as an external application on the surface of the life of the believer. It is not until you chew, eat, and swallow Scripture in the depth of your being that change will begin to come and the right foundation for prayer is built.

The basic idea of all Biblical Meditation is thinking repetitively on and about the Scriptures. The Hebrew word used most often for meditation comes from a cow chewing its cud. The cow bites off grass or hay and then proceeds to chew it until it is a gum-like substance. The cow continues to bite and chew this ball of partially chewed grass until it has released much of its nutrients. The cow then swallows the cud, depositing it into one of its stomachs. At some latter point the cow brings that cud back up and chews it some more, mixing it with new grass. More nutrients are released because of the new grass and because the stomach juices have broken the materials down further.

I am personally troubled by how few Christians have ever even heard about Biblical Meditation. In some Christian circles anything with the name meditation is seen as bad and to be avoided. Yet the Bible says that this single practice is the key to Christ-like life change. I get angry when I notice that eastern religions are demanding their adherents set aside three times per day to practice their form of meditation and Christians have never even heard of Biblical Meditation. We have the living and active Word of God, the crucified and risen Savior, the active presence of the Holy Spirit, and we are afraid to do what the Bible clearly tells us to do. Biblical Meditation is the most power injecting, peace inducing thing you can do every day. (Colossians 3:16) Don't miss this. Meditate on the Scriptures every day. Set aside time to do this, everyday.

There is such richness in Scripture that it can be read, studied, prayed, and confessed over and over again and there is still life, energy, and insights to be gained. This is what I was doing by slowly repeating Psalms 1 over and over. I was chewing the words and letters of the Scriptures to release the nutrients, power, and transformational concepts into my soul. There was so much energy locked in those words and concepts that I was able to feed off of this one Scripture for over three months.

The following are eleven of the ways of meditating (praying) on the Bible: slow repetition of the Bible; memorization of the Bible; study of the Bible; singing the Bible; confessing the Bible; praying the Bible; envisioning the Bible; personalizing the Bible; journaling your interactions with the Bible; diagram or analogize the Bible; and personal translation of the Bible. It is very helpful to become acquainted with all of these ways of injecting the biblical content into one's soul. There will be times during your spiritual journey when your favorite way will become dry and unable to supply you with the nutrients you need. It is at those times that we need to shift to a different way of seeking the Lord's face through Biblical Meditation. It is a shame that some people when going through difficulty just stop drawing the power of God into their lives and start pretending that everything is okay. Learn to pray in new ways through Biblical Meditation.

We experience God and enjoy transformative prayer through Biblical Meditation. Because this is true, let me remind you of two facts.

First, the power of God is injected into our life from the Bible, not books about the Bible. There are many great books about the Bible which are helpful, inspirational, joy-producing, and powerful. And while I get tremendous encouragement and help from books I read, it is the Bible itself and engagement with it that brings the power of God into a life.

Secondly, the power of God is always transformational and never ceremonial or empty showmanship. God does not give us power so we can "rev" our spiritual engines or "flex" our spiritual muscles. God wants our time in prayer in His word to actually result in love and change. Some people are more interested in looking spiritually powerful than actually making righteous changes. God does not empower people to do that. He gives us power to do real work in the real world. Therefore if God is going to release His power, it is going to bring about change.

Personal engagement with the Bible will unleash the living Word of God in your life. As we saw from Jesus in John 15:7, Biblical Meditation is the key to prayer being answered. Biblical Meditation is prayer at a deep and fundamental level. Biblical Meditation is the best part of prayer – it is listening to God speak. Things will begin to happen in and around you that would not have happened if you had not started to pray in this unique way. Biblical Meditation is not entertainment; it is injecting a new power source into your life so that you can achieve what you could never achieve on your own.

HOW TO GET STARTED PRAYING IN THIS NEW WAY: GREAT VERSES

Instead of thinking of prayer as reciting a laundry list of your wants to God and calling it prayer, start praying by reading the following Scriptures slowly out loud as you go to bed at night and/or sit comfortably in a chair during a break in your day. Some of these are single verses and some are extended sections. When I started praying this way, I did nothing more than just slowly repeat the words of Scripture as I went to bed. That exercise eventually led to my memorizing the passage, studying the passage, praying the passage, journaling about the passage, and envisioning the passage. Some of the various techniques for meditation will work better for some people than others. But slow repetition is a good place to start. I am asked from time to time which Scriptures to meditate upon. Let me give you a starter list I have put together. Put a check mark by the Scripture when you have meditated upon it.

Psa 1:1-3	Phil 1:6	Jam 1:26	1 John 2:15-18
1 John 2:1,2	1 John 3:1-3	Eph 6:1-4	2 Tim 3:16
Col 1:8-10	John 3:16	Col 3:10-12	Ex 20:1-17
Phil 2:1-10	Rom 8:28,29	1 Cor 3:13	2 Cor 10:5
James 1:2-5	1 Thess 4:3-5	Rom 6:1-6	Rom 6:11-16
Gal 5:16	Gal 5:22-25	Col 3:1,2,5,12	2 Pet 1:5-8
Heb 12:1,2	Gen 1:26	Heb 12:4,6,11	Psa 19:14

Page 23

Matt 28:18-20	Psa 119:9-11	Ex 34:6,7	Rom 11:33
1 Tim 6:15,16	Pro 23:4,5	1 Thess 5:23	Rev 20:11-15
Rev 22:12-14	Rev 21:1,2	Eph 4:11-13	Col 1:9-12
John 14:16,17	Heb 4:14-16	Rev 20:6	2 Cor 5:10

Realize that each Scripture is like a vitamin pill that releases all kinds of nutrients, minerals, and essential elements into your system. You can't tell how powerful a verse is until you have meditated upon it.

Let the sermon at church be the beginning of your own personal meditation on an individual Scripture. The pastor has already meditated on that Scripture and shared what he found through his meditation. Now it is your turn to meditate on Scripture and let God speak to you directly out of His Word. This will allow you to pray and seek God's presence in this new direction.

Sometimes you should take a verse of Scripture through each one of the meditation methods. This allows your spirit, mind, will, emotions, and body to be impacted by the particular Scripture. Sometimes you only need to go through a few of the meditation prayer methods.

Realize that every significant spiritual person in the history of the world has meditated on the Bible: Moses, David, Augustine, Paul, Anselm. David is one of the prime Scriptural examples of the transformative power of Biblical Meditation. David is called a man after God's own heart because he has pursued God's thinking and ideas. David was a young teenage boy who desperately wanted to know the way God thought, reasoned, and acted. So he, David, began memorizing and meditating upon the first five books of Moses, which was the only Bible he had. He repeated it slowly, he sang about it, and he put it up against his life. He pictured himself living out what the Scripture held as an ideal; he prayed it. In the middle of the night while watching his father's sheep, he began an intimate relationship with God. God rewarded this man -- because he wanted to think like God -- with the Kingship of Israel. His prayer life was consumed with how to think God's thoughts. He filled his mind with the Scriptures and God rewarded him in numerous ways.

Many of the greatest books of all time are really the result of prayerful Biblical Meditation. The biblical book of Psalms is a record of some of the songs that King David and others composed after memorizing and meditating on truths in the first five books of Moses. The book Pilgrims Progress was a product of John Bunyan's meditation on the Scriptures while he was confined in prison for preaching the gospel without a license. The Confessions of St Augustine is considered a classic of ancient literature and is really Augustine meditating on demands of Scripture and the places where he fell short of God's ideal. The book Institutes of the Christian Religion is the meditations on particular passages in Scriptures; a focus on the sovereignty of God by John Calvin. The book Spiritual Exercise by Ignatius Loyola is a book about cleansing the soul through prayer and picturing various scenes from the life of Jesus recorded in the gospels.

In the following pages I will detail with practical steps how to pray through various ways of Biblical Meditation. The main thing is that the Word of God is drilled deep into your mind and heart and your interaction with God (prayer life) deepens based upon the Scripture and not your subjective experience. You will find some forms of meditations that really open up the Word of God for you; others that do not move you. It may be that years from now or in response to a particular life event, some of the methods that leave you unmoved will jump to life with new meaning.

	Date: _____
Scripture	_____
Slow Repetition	_____
Memorization	_____
Study	_____
Singing	_____
Confessing	_____
Praying	_____
Envisioning	_____
Personalize	_____
Journal Insights	_____
Diagramming/ Analogy	_____
Personal Translation	_____

	Date: _____
Scripture	
Slow Repetition	
Memorization	
Study	
Singing	
Confessing	
Praying	
Envisioning	
Personalize	
Journal Insights	
Diagramming/ Analogy	
Personal Translation	

SLOW REPETITION OF THE BIBLE
1 Timothy 4:13; 2 Timothy 3:15; Deuteronomy 17:19

In this form of Biblical Meditation and prayer you are pressing Scripture through your mind, will, and emotions. The slow repetition of the same ideas causes your mind to begin asking questions about the text. It causes your emotions to react to certain truths and commands. It challenges your will to adapt and submit to the word of God the more you say it and understand its implications. This is such a powerful form of pushing God's Word into the depth of your being. It is from in your soul that God's living active word can begin to do its work. He challenges us. He encourages us. He empowers us. It is all prayer at its most fundamental and dynamic best.

As I explained at the beginning of this book, Biblical Meditation is how I was told to begin releasing the power of God in my life. It was not called prayer. It was just what serious Christians did if they wanted to have God's power at work in their life. Memorize a section of Scripture and start saying it slowly over and over again. Your thinking about and speaking the Scripture is a prayer. You can do this anywhere. I was taught to do it as you lay in your bed before sleep comes over you. You should do this in a comfortable place where you will be able to completely relax as you focus on Scripture. Say the words out loud even though they maybe barely audible. I find that at times I am mouthing the words of Scripture with little or no sound coming out of my mouth. It seems best to not just say them in your head. It is harder to stay focused when you are only saying them in your head. The mind can too easily wander to the events of the day or the bills or the television program you just watched. The idea is to focus on the words of Scripture and put them between the teeth of your soul and bite down until the nutrients and power are broken free from the letters. As you are saying each word, use different inflections. This will give a slightly different meaning or angle to the verse. This will allow you to get new insights and understanding about the verse. As you are slowly saying the words, ask yourself and God questions about the words, phrases, concepts, and ideas that are in the verse. In one sense you will be beginning a dialogue with the author of Scripture. What did He put in this verse? Why did He put it there? What does this Scripture have to do with you? As you do this you will find yourself thinking about things in Scripture, life, relationships, and the future that you would never have thought about without this exercise.

If your mind wanders off of the Scripture or thoughts related to the Scripture, then bring your mind back. Usually it can be brought back by saying the Scripture slowly again. I may end up saying a Scripture dozens of times during a period of Biblical Meditation. For some people it becomes almost impossible to not have a pencil and paper nearby to capture their thoughts, insights, and interactions with the Lord.

How To Make Prayer Work

Biblical Meditation and Prayer Exercise

Let me suggest that you slowly repeat your favorite Scripture or one of the verses that are listed below or one of the classic passages of the Scriptures.

Psa 1:1-3	Phil 1:6	Jam 1:26	1 John 2:15-18
1 John 2:1,2	1 John 3:1-3	Eph 6:1-4	2 Tim 3:16
Col 1:8-10	John 3:16	Col 3:10-12	Ex 20:1-17
Phil 2:1-10	Rom 8:28,29	1 Cor 3:13	2 Cor 10:5
James 1:2-5	1 Thess 4:3-5	Rom 6:1-6	Rom 6:11-16
Gal 5:16	Gal 5:22-25	Col 3:1,2,5,12	2 Pet 1:5-8
Heb 12:1,2	Gen 1:26	Heb 12:4,6,11	Psa 19:14
Matt 28:18-20	Psa 119:9-11	Ex 34:6,7	Rom 11:33
1 Tim 6:15,16	Pro 23:4,5	1 Thess 5:23	Rev 20:11-15
Rev 22:12-14	Rev 21:1,2	Eph 4:11-13	Col 1:9-12
John 14:16,17	Heb 4:14-16	Rev 20:6	2 Cor 5:10

I find that repeating key verses of the Scriptures over each day helps quite a bit. They key Scriptures that I repeat every day are The Lord's Prayer, The Ladder of Virtue, The Fruit of the Spirit, The First and Second Great Commandments, The Ten Commandments, and The Beatitudes. I repeat them slowly and prayerfully. I know I can say them at any time as a refresher as to what God is trying to do in my life.

I have the habit of saying these in the shower while I stretch using various stretching exercises. I have these key verses laminated so I can read them off. I have recently added a short definition to the qualities mentioned. I have added them in the form of affirmations of what I want God to do in me as I go forward with

Him. It is amazing how the Holy Spirit moves me toward the goals mentioned in these Scriptures because I say them every day.

I have put these on separate pages so that you can copy them or laminate them and begin repeating them as a part of your every day routine.

The Lord's Prayer

Our Father,
who art in heaven
Hallowed be Thy Name
Thy Kingdom come
Thy will be done on earth
as it is in heaven
Give us this day our daily bread
And forgive us our trespasses
as we forgive those
who trespass against us
Lead us not into temptation
but deliver us from evil
For Thine is the Kingdom
and the Power and the Glory
Forever and ever
Amen

The Fruit of the Spirit

The fruit of the Spirit is
Love, Joy, Peace, Patience, Kindness, Goodness,
Meekness, Faithfulness, and, Self-Control
against such things there is no law.

The Ladder of Virtue

… applying all diligence,
in your faith supply moral excellence,
and in your moral excellence, knowledge,
and in your knowledge, self-control,
and in your self-control, perseverance,
and in your perseverance, godliness,
and in your godliness, brotherly kindness,
and in your brotherly kindness,
Christian love.
For if these qualities are yours
and are increasing,
they render you neither useless
nor unfruitful in the true knowledge
of our Lord Jesus Christ.

First and Second Great Commandments

You shall love
the Lord your God
with all your heart, soul, mind and strength
And
Your neighbor as yourself

The Ten Commandments

You shall have no other gods before Me.
You shall not make for yourselves
any graven images.
You shall not take the Name of
the Lord your God in vain.
Remember the Sabbath day to keep it holy.
Honor your Father and your Mother.
You shall not murder.
You shall not commit adultery.
You shall not steal.
You shall not bear false witness
against your neighbor.
You shall not covet anything that
belongs to your neighbor.

The Beatitudes

Blessed are the poor in spirit, for theirs is the kingdom of heaven.
Blessed are those who mourn, for they shall be comforted.
Blessed are the meek, for they shall inherit the earth.
Blessed are those who hunger and thirst for righteousness, for they shall be satisfied.
Blessed are the merciful, for they shall receive mercy.
Blessed are the pure in heart, for they shall see God.
Blessed are the peacemakers, for they shall be called sons of God.
Blessed are those who have been persecuted for the sake of righteousness, for theirs is the kingdom of heaven.
Blessed are you when people insult you and persecute you, and falsely say all kinds of evil against you because of Me.
Rejoice and be glad, for your reward in heaven is great; for in the same way they persecuted the prophets who were before you.

Memorization of the Bible
Psalm 119:10,11

Just the title of this chapter is scaring many of you. Do not let the idea of memorizing Scripture scare you. I have had many people tell me that they can't memorize anything. They use the techniques that I share in this chapter and start memorizing verses and phrases of God's word. They get so excited and God begins to do His work. I have even heard of people who have had their brains pretty well fried from drugs and alcohol and be able to rebuild focus and clarity of thought through Biblical Meditation and memorization.

Another way of meditating on the Bible is to memorize Scripture. Here the emphasis is not upon repeating the verse slowly as to have the Scripture in one's head. In this method one is again pressing Scripture into one's mind. It is getting a verse of Scripture into one's soul for God's Spirit to use. When we have to look up a Scripture to remember any part of it, it is only externally applied to our life. Get the Scriptures into your soul. It is very valuable in trying to sense the leading of the Holy Spirit to give the Spirit of God a greater amount of vocabulary to guide us. When we memorize the Scripture and know the biblical stories, God can bring a verse to mind or a story from Scripture. God the Holy Spirit can speak to our soul that we are about to face a situation like Joshua when he faced the city of Ai. He can remind us that we need to behave like the Bereans. The Holy Spirit may whisper Philippians 1:6 in our spirit when we are tempted to give up and give into sin. Realize that if you do not know the Scriptures, then your ability to "hear" from the Lord will be severely hampered.

    I memorize a new verse of Scriptures every day. Whatever verse that I am reading or studying that day. As I read and study, God always highlights a particular verse or phrase which seems to be where I need to focus for that day. It is that verse or that phrase that I say out loud a number of times until it is memorized. Often just the process of studying it causes me to have it memorized. I will try and say it throughout the day or write it on a card that I can put in my pocket or attach to the visor of my car. My goal is to be able to remember that verse or phrase at the end of the day. If I can remember the verse or phrase at the end of the day without looking, then I meditated on the verse and God has been changing me. I do not try and remember it past that one day. I let it go and go on to the next verse that God will highlight in my devotional time.

    Some people do not put much time into memorizing Scripture because they can't remember what they memorize forever. I tell my seminary students that you don't have to remember the Scriptures that you memorize. Once you get the Scriptures in your soul, God can bring them back to mind whenever He wants. In the book of Isaiah, God compares Scripture that has been memorized to a snow bank that He can melt at any time and send a stream of fresh water through your life. I try to memorize and repeat a new verse of Scripture every day. If you ask me what verse I memorized last week or two weeks ago, I could probably not tell you. My goal is to be able to say the verse of Scripture at the conclusion of the day. If I have carried around one verse of Scripture all day and thought about it in different ways, then the day has been successful. Memorizing Scripture is like throwing mud against the wall. The more you throw the more will hopefully stick and eventually the wall will be covered.

Probably the best way to memorize the Scripture that I have found is to just read the verse out loud slowly ten times. Do not try and memorize it; just focus on it while you are reading it out loud. Usually by the fifth time you can say major parts of it without looking. By the eighth time you can say the whole thing without looking. By the tenth time you have it down so that fifteen minutes later you can say it again without looking. You have this Scripture now inside your soul ready to be used by the Lord whenever He wants to use it.

I had the privilege when I was growing up of having an amazing youth pastor. He constantly had me memorizing and meditating on various biblical passages. He taught and reinforced many of these biblical habits in my life. I want to act like that kind of coach in your life through this book. Do not put down this book because you don't want to do this or you don't think you can. Read to the end of this chapter and do at least one of the memorization exercises. There were a number of occasions where my youth pastor made me memorize whole chapters of the Scriptures and recite them to him. I remember memorizing 1 John chapter 2 especially. It took me a number of weeks to finish memorizing. He would listen each week as I would forget certain sections or miss words and just kept pressing me to memorize the whole thing. He also wanted me to present to him ten pages of insights and meditations on that chapter when I had finished memorizing 1 John 2. His requirement of a higher level of Christian commitment and his willingness to listen to me recite the Scriptures changed the way I think because the Scriptures were in my conscious and unconscious mind doing their work.

Biblical Meditation and Prayer Exercise

You might start with this list of verses and begin memorizing one of the verses or the whole section. Remember it is okay if you can only remember it for one day or a few days. You can always go back and re-memorize it. And the Holy Spirit can bring it back to your memory. Just repeat a Scripture out loud slowly ten times, and it will probably be memorized for a day. Once it is in your soul, it is in there. Do not worry if you can't remember the Scripture that you memorized a few days back. It is in there. Just keep moving.

Psa 1:1-3	Phil 1:6	Jam 1:26	1 John 2:15-18
1 John 2:1,2	1 John 3:1-3	Eph 6:1-4	2 Tim 3:16
Col 1:8-10	John 3:16	Col 3:10-12	Ex 20:1-17
Phil 2:1-10	Rom 8:28,29	1 Cor 3:13	2 Cor 10:5
James 1:2-5	1 Thess 4:3-5	Rom 6:1-6	Rom 6:11-16
Gal 5:16	Gal 5:22-25	Col 3:1,2,5,12	2 Pet 1:5-8
Heb 12:1,2	Gen 1:26	Heb 12:4,6,11	Psa 19:14
Matt 28:18-20	Psa 119:9-11	Ex 34:6,7	Rom 11:33
1 Tim 6:15,16	Pro 23:4,5	1 Thess 5:23	Rev 20:11-15
Rev 22:12-14	Rev 21:1,2	Eph 4:11-13	Col 1:9-12
John 14:16,17	Heb 4:14-16	Rev 20:6	2 Cor 5:10

	Date: _____
Scripture	
Slow Repetition	
Memorization	
Study	
Singing	
Confessing	
Praying	
Envisioning	
Personalize	
Journal Insights	
Diagramming/ Analogy	
Personal Translation	

	Date: _____
Scripture	
Slow Repetition	
Memorization	
Study	
Singing	
Confessing	
Praying	
Envisioning	
Personalize	
Journal Insights	
Diagramming/ Analogy	
Personal Translation	

	Date:
Scripture	
Slow Repetition	
Memorization	
Study	
Singing	
Confessing	
Praying	
Envisioning	
Personalize	
Journal Insights	
Diagramming/ Analogy	
Personal Translation	

Memorization Of The Bible

	Date:
Scripture	
Slow Repetition	
Memorization	
Study	
Singing	
Confessing	
Praying	
Envisioning	
Personalize	
Journal Insights	
Diagramming/ Analogy	
Personal Translation	

STUDY OF THE BIBLE
2 Timothy 2:15; 4:13

    This is probably my favorite form of prayer. It is the listening part. God speaks through His word. He has spoken, and He will speak to us directly as we take the time to study His word. Our world, and even some Christians, are seeking desperately to hear from beyond our realm. God has spoken to us and it is recorded in written form as the Bible. The Bible is a treasure of unimagined value. It is the communication of God. It is alive, authoritative, and discerning (Hebrews 4:12). Prayer is a conversation with God and studying the depth of His Word is where He speaks clearly back to us. In this method of biblical meditation we are breaking open the wonders of God's communication with us. This presses the Scriptures again deeper and deeper into our soul: mind, will, and emotions. This discipline will take time, but it is one of the best forms of prayer. It is learning, listening, and being led by God Himself in prayer. It does not get much better than this.

    Studying the Bible is not a complicated process; it involves three steps. First, observing the passage; second, interpreting the passage; and third applying the passage. These three steps allow any passage to open up before you. The meaning of the text will become evident as you study the context, the words, the culture, and the cross references. The Bible is not a mystery book which is incomprehensible to the common person. God communicated with His people in a way that they can understand. If we follow the normal rules for understanding any kind of written communication, we can comprehend what God is saying to us.

Let's take a look at what is involved in observing a passage. First, read the passage over a few times. Second, write out every word of the passage you want to study on a separate sheet of paper (in the journal pages of this book); highlight important words (make them bigger or smaller in relative size); show relationships between ideas (put important thoughts in the center of the page and explanatory thoughts to the side), displaying which phrases are explanatory and which ones are the main points. Third, circle key words in the passage and write down questions that come to mind as you investigate the verse.

When you begin interpreting a passage, you define key words in an English dictionary or biblical dictionary.
Second, look for important background information about the time, place, circumstances, author, and recipients of the section you are studying. Third, check cross references to your verse if there are any. Fourth, answer the questions that you have written, if you can. Fifth, look at commentaries for further information about your passage.

Applying the passage to your life is the point of doing a Bible study as Biblical Meditation. There are three possible applications for any verse: Know, Feel, and/or Do.

Ask and answer:
1. What does God want me to know because of this passage?
2. What does God want me to feel because of this passage?
3. What does God want me to do because of this passage?

Further application questions might be:
Why has God led me to this passage today?
Why does God want me to know, feel, or do this verse today?

Studying the Bible in some cases has become so specialized that it is no longer seen as Biblical Meditation. It is true if one is studying a passage for academic purposes or solely to teach its content to others with no personal application or engagement, then studying the Bible is not Biblical Meditation.

There is such richness in the Bible that only study of it will let you see it and interact with God about it. I highly recommend doing Bible study every day. I find that I have almost become addicted to Bible study every day. The simple practices mentioned above, which were taught by my youth pastor, bring God's truth to me every day.

Biblical Meditation and Prayer Exercise

Begin by studying one of your favorite passages of Scripture or one of the classic passages that you have been slowly repeating or one of the passages listed below.

Psa 1:1-3	Phil 1:6	Jam 1:26	1 John 2:15-18
1 John 2:1,2	1 John 3:1-3	Eph 6:1-4	2 Tim 3:16
Col 1:8-10	John 3:16	Col 3:10-12	Ex 20:1-17
Phil 2:1-10	Rom 8:28,29	1 Cor 3:13	2 Cor 10:5
James 1:2-5	1 Thess 4:3-5	Rom 6:1-6	Rom 6:11-16
Gal 5:16	Gal 5:22-25	Col 3:1,2,5,12	2 Pet 1:5-8
Heb 12:1,2	Gen 1:26	Heb 12:4,6,11	Psa 19:14
Matt 28:18-20	Psa 119:9-11	Ex 34:6,7	Rom 11:33
1 Tim 6:15,16	Pro 23:4,5	1 Thess 5:23	Rev 20:11-15
Rev 22:12-14	Rev 21:1,2	Eph 4:11-13	Col 1:9-12
John 14:16,17	Heb 4:14-16	Rev 20:6	2 Cor 5:10

Study Of The Bible

	Date: _____
Scripture	
Slow Repetition	
Memorization	
Study	
Singing	
Confessing	
Praying	
Envisioning	
Personalize	
Journal Insights	
Diagramming/ Analogy	
Personal Translation	

	Date: _____
Scripture	
Slow Repetition	
Memorization	
Study	
Singing	
Confessing	
Praying	
Envisioning	
Personalize	
Journal Insights	
Diagramming/ Analogy	
Personal Translation	

SINGING THE BIBLE
Ephesians 5:19; Colossians 3:17; Psalms

In this form of Biblical Meditation you are pressing the Scriptures through your emotions. Singing seems to often bypass the conscious mind and engage the emotions and unconscious mind directly. This form of meditation is often avoided or dismissed as childish, but it is very powerful in pushing Scripture deep into your being. Yes, it is funny to hear yourself start singing, especially if you don't have a great voice. But it can be so powerful in releasing ones emotions and pouring Scripture into the place of our feelings and reactions.

I have assigned this form of prayer to many young leaders who wanted to increase their leadership. They often shy away from this discipline because it is so foreign to our culture. But many try it and find they are tapping into a deep vein of Scripture and their own emotion in a very powerful way. A number have told me that it always brought a smile or a laugh to their life and allowed them to verbalize a truth they needed or expose a feeling that was somewhat hidden. Don't skip over this practice of prayer. Leaders that God uses are willing to expose themselves to God even down to the core of their emotions and reactions. It is this naked exposure of our soul to God and His Word that moves us forward as a spiritual leader.

There are a few directions that this fascinating way of meditating on the Bible can go. One is where a tune is invented, manipulated, or concocted to fit the exact words of Scripture. A second way of singing the Bible is to paraphrase a biblical text and set it to a powerful melody. A third way of singing the Bible is to take a biblical idea or concept and set it to music.

Each of these three ways of meditating on the Bible through singing can be enjoyed in two different ways. First, you can build your own original compositions. If you are not musically creative or gifted, then you may not want to have anyone around when you try this but do not fail to try. It does not matter that what you created is awful musically; it matters that you are thinking about Scripture in new ways. The process of singing opens you up emotionally in new ways. This allows the Scriptures to penetrate deep into the crevices and secret places of your life.

The second way you can enjoy singing the Bible as Biblical Meditation is to find artists who have done all the work for you. They have put actual Scripture verses to creative, beautiful, and listenable melodies. They have paraphrased Scripture and married this to interesting tunes. They have taken truly biblical concepts and wove them into powerful lyrics set to good music. When you find music like this, purchase it and listen to it over and over again.

Shortly after I became a Christian, I was impressed by God to turn off the radio when I was in the car and sing the Scriptures that I had been memorizing. I sang Psalm 1:1-3 and Ephesians 1:18-23. Those were the only verses I had memorized at the time. I was glad I was alone but as I tried to sing the Scriptures to this tune I was making up, joy began to well up inside of me and I could not help but smile and laugh. I may have laughed at how ridiculous I sounded, but the joy was unexpected and incredibly delightful. It seems that music and singing bypasses the intellectual side of our minds and moves very quickly to our soul and spirit. It has been said that all music is meditation and touches the soul.

Even though this will be awkward and most likely not for public consumption, turn the radio off and sing whatever Scriptures that you have memorized and enjoy the soul connection with the author of the Bible. I think you will be amazed at what happens.

Go ahead and sing your favorite Bible passage right now. It doesn't have to be pretty or even be in tune. Put a passage to music. "For God so loved the world that He gave His only begotten Son that whosoever believeth in Him shall not perish but have everlasting life." Sing this famous verse.

Too often we are caught up in the idea that it will be embarrassing or people will laugh at us. But this is prayer to God. It is between you and God. He thinks it wonderful that you are speaking His words back to Him. He will respond.

Sing the truths in the following passages. "There is therefore no condemnation for those who are in Christ Jesus." Romans 8:1. Make up a song about the truth of freedom from condemnation in Jesus. "My little children, I write these things to you that you may not sin, but if any one does sin, we have an advocate with the Father, Jesus Christ the righteous. And He Himself is the propitiation for our sins and not for ours only but also for those of the whole world." 1 John 2:1,2 Start singing about how there is an answer to sins that we commit. It is Jesus. He is our defense attorney.

Start singing the problems that you are facing, asking God to bring Scripture to your mind that you can read, pray, sing, study, and abide in to find the answers. Singing opens a direct channel to our soul. Your soul does not know how to deal with the problems it is facing but God does, and He has revealed the answers in the Scriptures. Singing allows you to open your soul to God and His words.

Biblical Meditation and Prayer Exercise

The following are various sections of Scripture that you might choose to meditate on through singing. Write down the passage on a separate sheet or paper or on a 3x5 card and attach it to the visor in your car. Many times the only time we can convince our self to sing is when we are alone driving the car. This is great. The other time is in the shower and the water will muffle our voice. But then the card needs to be laminated. Just try this it will be a great blessing in your life.

Psa 1:1-3	Phil 1:6	Jam 1:26	1 John 2:15-18
1 John 2:1,2	1 John 3:1-3	Eph 6:1-4	2 Tim 3:16
Col 1:8-10	John 3:16	Col 3:10-12	Ex 20:1-17
Phil 2:1-10	Rom 8:28,29	1 Cor 3:13	2 Cor 10:5
James 1:2-5	1 Thess 4:3-5	Rom 6:1-6	Rom 6:11-16
Gal 5:16	Gal 5:22-25	Col 3:1,2,5,12	2 Pet 1:5-8
Heb 12:1,2	Gen 1:26	Heb 12:4,6,11	Psa 19:14
Matt 28:18-20	Psa 119:9-11	Ex 34:6,7	Rom 11:33
1 Tim 6:15,16	Pro 23:4,5	1 Thess 5:23	Rev 20:11-15
Rev 22:12-14	Rev 21:1,2	Eph 4:11-13	Col 1:9-12
John 14:16,17	Heb 4:14-16	Rev 20:6	2 Cor 5:10

	Date: _____
Scripture	_____
Slow Repetition	_____
Memorization	_____
Study	_____
Singing	_____
Confessing	_____
Praying	_____
Envisioning	_____
Personalize	_____
Journal Insights	_____
Diagramming/ Analogy	_____
Personal Translation	_____

	Date: _____
Scripture	
Slow Repetition	
Memorization	
Study	
Singing	
Confessing	
Praying	
Envisioning	
Personalize	
Journal Insights	
Diagramming/ Analogy	
Personal Translation	

CONFESSING THE BIBLE
Nehemiah 9; Daniel 9; Deuteronomy 27

The process of confessing the Bible is a little different than confessing your sins. In this form of Biblical Meditation and prayer you are pressing Scripture through your will. You are forcing your will to acknowledge the truth of Scripture both positively and negatively. Too often when we see a Scripture that we are uncomfortable with, we just keep reading or skip over it because we are uncomfortable with what it says. We never make our will come to grips with the ideas, commands, or implications of that Scripture. In this step you are not going to let that happen anymore. Your will must adapt to Scripture; it must submit. Life change demands that our rebellious nature will not continue to win. For these reasons, this form of Biblical Meditation and prayer is overlooked and/ or purposely ignored. Yet so much of the abundant life that God has for us is missed if we will not submit to His will for us and we insist on major areas of rebellion in our life.

When you are confessing the Bible, you are using a Bible verse or a Bible section and combing through it for places where you completely agree with the truth or action presented in that verse. To confess is to agree with God regarding something. In this first case you are agreeing about a positive. You are interacting with God based upon the verse or section of the Bible you are looking at. You speak out your agreement: "God, I agree with you that you are

Sovereign and the only Lord." "I have placed you as Lord in my life and the only truly wise God of all my decisions." Or "Dear God, I agree with you that a man must be willing to lay down his life for his wife, just as you did for your church." "I ask you to show me any area where I am not doing that so that I may be in more complete agreement with this truth."

The second type of confessing of the Bible is agreeing with God when you do not measure up to a truth or righteous action. There is tremendous power released for life change when we admit that a specific action, belief, or pattern is not right. We cut the invisible spiritual, mental, emotional, and relational cords when we confess these negative aspects of our life. We cannot move forward with positive life change until we have been released from what has been holding us back. We may not have even been thinking about something that the Scripture clearly is pointing out. But when the Scripture is clear and our lives don't measure up, then it is time to confess.

This particular Biblical Meditation technique is the one that God used to convince me that I should marry the woman who became my wife. She was clearly an outstanding woman of wisdom, virtue, and beauty as I got to know her; but I was not convinced that she was the one. Something was missing. We were dating and things were going well, but one of the key things that I was looking for in a woman was the ability to philosophize and carry on abstract debate. Dana is godly, humble, adaptable, smart, beautiful, enjoyable, and wise; but she did not philosophize at all. I remember praying for a week that this probably was not the one because of this missing ingredient. I had built up this ability to be one of the most important things I was looking for in a wife.

In a time of prayer God brought me to the Proverbs where it says that wisdom is above all things and nothing you desire compares to wisdom (Proverbs 3:13-18). It is better than silver or precious stones. It was like He was directly asking me whether Dana was wise. I replied that she was. Well then, seemed to be the response, isn't wisdom above philosophizing? I had to confess that I was not being biblical in my list of qualities I was looking for. I bowed my head and wept as I confessed how I had made a false standard as important as a biblical one and almost missed the most awesome woman that God had brought my way. After pressing this Scripture through my will in confession, I was able to realize what a true gift she was and I began making wedding plans.

Biblical Meditation and Prayer Exercise

Take a favorite passage and/or one that deals with a problem you are facing and move through this confession exercise or one from the list below:

Psa 1:1-3	Phil 1:6	Jam 1:26	1 John 2:15-18
1 John 2:1,2	1 John 3:1-3	Eph 6:1-4	2 Tim 3:16
Col 1:8-10	John 3:16	Col 3:10-12	Ex 20:1-17
Phil 2:1-10	Rom 8:28,29	1 Cor 3:13	2 Cor 10:5
James 1:2-5	1 Thess 4:3-5	Rom 6:1-6	Rom 6:11-16
Gal 5:16	Gal 5:22-25	Col 3:1,2,5,12	2 Pet 1:5-8
Heb 12:1,2	Gen 1:26	Heb 12:4,6,11	Psa 19:14
Matt 28:18-20	Psa 119:9-11	Ex 34:6,7	Rom 11:33
1 Tim 6:15,16	Pro 23:4,5	1 Thess 5:23	Rev 20:11-15
Rev 22:12-14	Rev 21:1,2	Eph 4:11-13	Col 1:9-12
John 14:16,17	Heb 4:14-16	Rev 20:6	2 Cor 5:10

Ask yourself the following questions:

What truths are in this passage that I completely agree with?
What truths in this passage have I not fully embraced?
What truths in this passage am I against?

What actions in this verse am I already doing?
What truths do I ignore or completely disagree with?
Do any of my actions violate this verse?

The Christian's Position in Christ

I am God's child. John 1:12
I am Christ's friend. John 15:15
I have been justified. Romans 5:1
I am united and I am one spirit with the Lord. 1 Corinthians 6:7
I have been bought with a price. 1 Corinthians 6:20
I belong to God. 1 Corinthians 6:19,20
I have been adopted as God's child. Ephesians 1:5
I have been forgiven of all my sins and redeemed. Colossians 1:14
I am free from condemnation. Romans 8:1,2
I know that all things work together for good. Romans 8:28
I cannot be separated from the love of God. Romans 8:35
I have been anointed and sealed by God. 2 Corinthians 1:21,22
I am confident that God will continue to work on me.
  Philippians 1:6
I am a citizen of heaven. Philippians 3:20
I have a spirit of power, love, and a sound mind, not fear.
  2 Timothy 1:7
I can approach God and find grace and mercy. Hebrews 4:16
The Evil One cannot own me. 1 John 5:18
I am the salt and light of the earth. Matthew 5:13,14
I have been chosen to bear fruit. John 15:16
I will receive power to witness for Christ. Acts 1:8
I am God's temple. 1 Corinthians 6:19
I am a minister of reconciliation. 2 Corinthians 5:17
I am God's co-worker. 1 Corinthians 3:9; 2 Corinthians 6:1
I am seated with Christ in heaven. Ephesians 2:6
I am God's workmanship. Ephesians 2:10
I approach God with freedom and confidence. Ephesians 3:12
I can do all things through Christ. Philippians 4:13

	Date: _____
Scripture	_____
Slow Repetition	_____
Memorization	_____
Study	_____
Singing	_____
Confessing	_____
Praying	_____
Envisioning	_____
Personalize	_____
Journal Insights	_____
Diagramming/ Analogy	_____
Personal Translation	_____

Ten Commandments

You shall have no other gods before Me
I make sure that nothing is a higher value in my life than God and my relationship with Him.

You shall not make for yourself any graven images
I do not allow misrepresentations of God to diminish my understanding or worship of Him.

You shall not take the name of the Lord your God in vain
I make sure that my words and actions do not reflect badly on God.

Remember the Sabbath Day to keep it holy
I worship God everyday as an individual and at least once a week in a group of sincere believers.

Honor your Father and your Mother
I add value to my parents through my speech, actions, and attitudes towards them.

You shall not murder
I do not use violence or anger to get my own way.

You shall not commit adultery
I remain faithful to the wife God has given me -- mentally and physically.

You shall not steal
I produce an abundance of money and goods through my work so that I can be generous with those in need.

You shall not bear false witness against your neighbor
I speak the truth in love and do not deceive or manipulate the truth to suit my purposes.

You shall not covet anything that belongs to your neighbor
I look for God's gifts and blessing to me rather than envying the blessings of someone else.

	Date: _____
Scripture	
Slow Repetition	
Memorization	
Study	
Singing	
Confessing	
Praying	
Envisioning	
Personalize	
Journal Insights	
Diagramming/ Analogy	
Personal Translation	

	Date:
Scripture	
Slow Repetition	
Memorization	
Study	
Singing	
Confessing	
Praying	
Envisioning	
Personalize	
Journal Insights	
Diagramming/ Analogy	
Personal Translation	

Confessing The Bible

	Date: _____
Scripture	_____
Slow Repetition	_____
Memorization	_____
Study	_____
Singing	_____
Confessing	_____
Praying	_____
Envisioning	_____
Personalize	_____
Journal Insights	_____
Diagramming/ Analogy	_____
Personal Translation	_____

	Date: _____
Scripture	_____
	_____
Slow Repetition	_____
	_____
Memorization	_____
	_____
Study	_____
	_____
Singing	_____
	_____
Confessing	_____
	_____
Praying	_____
	_____
Envisioning	_____
	_____
Personalize	_____
	_____
Journal Insights	_____
	_____
Diagramming/ Analogy	_____
	_____
Personal Translation	_____
	_____
	_____

PRAYING THE BIBLE

There are a number of ways of praying the Bible. All of these forms of Biblical Meditation presses the Scripture through your will and emotions. When you pray the Bible, you are forced to see the world God's way and ask Him for what is in the Scripture instead of looking at the world through your self-focused lenses asking for what you want. This is a way of allowing God to show you the world through His eyes. This method of praying may seem odd at first because you have to really adopt the Scriptures' point of view rather than your own.

One way made famous by George Mueller -- the man who funded his orphanages for the poor just on pray alone -- was to get on his knees every morning next to his bedside with his Bible open in front of him and begin prayerfully reading the Bible. He would ask for insight into verses, power to apply what he was reading, and deeper connection with God over the truths he was reading. There is also the practice of asking God for everything that is in a passage. For instance if one was meditating on Matthew 6:10 "Your kingdom come. Your will be done, On earth as it is in heaven." One might pray:

Dear Lord,
I want Your kingdom to come into my life in a new and powerful way. I desperately want to stop being plain old me. I want

you, Jesus, to invade my body, my life, and my thinking so it is no longer just me but You and Your direction for my life. I want Your kingdom of love and righteousness to fill my marriage. May my spouse see something different about me;, the unmistakable aroma of the Holy Spirit. I want Your love to fill me so that how I talk with her/him, how I act toward her/him, how I touch her/him is completely filled with love and joy. Cause me to see, Lord, how I can meet his/her real needs and empower him/her to change.

I ask You, Lord Jesus, to fill me with the joy, righteousness, and peace of Your kingdom so that everyone can see that I am a representative of a great King who has changed me. I ask you, God, to bring down Your kingdom into my family. Make my children sense your evaluating presence. Cause me to overflow with love for them in how I listen to them and react to them. Cause me to use my time, my money, and my energy in a way for my family to see how truly important they are to me.

Lord Jesus, I need a fresh infusion of You at my work. Make me not a Jesus freak but a humble, gracious, giving person who makes a positive difference where ever I go. Cause me to think, speak, and do things that will cause Your blessing on the business so my bosses will see what a Christian blessing is like.

Lord, bring the kingdom ministry to my church. Don't let us just spin our wheels, turning out services, speeches, and singing without truly exalting You or changing lives. Rock our church with Your presence. Lord Jesus, I need some new friends who will challenge me to be more for You and more for myself. Cause me to see the people who are willing to become my friends if I just put forth some effort. Cause me to see and give me the way to move away from friends who are pulling me away from You and Your desires for my life.

Open my eyes, Lord to the ways I can create more money and manage my money in such a way as to build lots of relational wealth that truly glorifies you. Lord Jesus, I want to tithe my income to Your work and become a generous person beyond just basic tithing; give me the faith, courage, and opportunities to make that happen. I do not want to just exist where I live, I want to make a difference. Bring the people, groups, needs across my path that I need to be supporting with my time, skills, energy, and money.

I want to live in harmony with Your plan for me even if that is at odds with my plans for me. I realize that I will not have the level of satisfaction, significance, and meaning I want until You and I are on the same page and singing from the same song book. Fill my life with Your love that I might overflow into other people's life and offer people a fresh evidence that God is still alive and active in our world.

Your Servant,

This is one way to turn a passage of Scripture into a prayer. Praying the Bible doesn't have to be fancy. It should just be an honest request to God for the truth of the Bible to become true for you and the people you know. Make sure that you listen for God's still small voice back to you as you are praying His Word.

I know of a very famous Christian author who used to spend Sunday afternoons alone praying through portions of the Bible and enjoying deep communion with God through that process. He says that it is what gives him the ability to keep his very busy schedule. It was out of those times of prayer that much of his writing grew.

Jesus tells us that God is seeking worshippers who will worship Him in spirit and truth. Praying the word is a way of making sure that our prayers are encased in the truth.

I know of some people who read and pray the Lord's Prayer every night as they go to bed. This is a simple repeatable way of getting ready for bed with Scripture on their mind as they go to bed. Some people read a new Psalm every night and then pray with their spouse about whatever that Psalm triggers in their mind.

Biblical Meditation and Prayer Exercise

Take one of your favorite passages of Scripture and/or one of the ones listed below and read through it and then begin praying for all that is in that passage. This would mean thanking God for what He has done, adoring who He is in the passage, asking for what God wants you to have from the passage, interceding for others about what is in the passage, confessing to God what you are getting right in the passage and what you are still needing to change.

Psa 1:1-3	Phil 1:6	Jam 1:26	1 John 2:15-18
1 John 2:1,2	1 John 3:1-3	Eph 6:1-4	2 Tim 3:16
Col 1:8-10	John 3:16	Col 3:10-12	Ex 20:1-17
Phil 2:1-10	Rom 8:28,29	1 Cor 3:13	2 Cor 10:5
James 1:2-5	1 Thess 4:3-5	Rom 6:1-6	Rom 6:11-16
Gal 5:16	Gal 5:22-25	Col 3:1,2,5,12	2 Pet 1:5-8
Heb 12:1,2	Gen 1:26	Heb 12:4,6,11	Psa 19:14
Matt 28:18-20	Psa 119:9-11	Ex 34:6,7	Rom 11:33
1 Tim 6:15,16	Pro 23:4,5	1 Thess 5:23	Rev 20:11-15
Rev 22:12-14	Rev 21:1,2	Eph 4:11-13	Col 1:9-12
John 14:16,17	Heb 4:14-16	Rev 20:6	2 Cor 5:10

Praying The Bible

	Date: _____
Scripture	
Slow Repetition	
Memorization	
Study	
Singing	
Confessing	
Praying	
Envisioning	
Personalize	
Journal Insights	
Diagramming/ Analogy	
Personal Translation	

	Date: _____
Scripture	
Slow Repetition	
Memorization	
Study	
Singing	
Confessing	
Praying	
Envisioning	
Personalize	
Journal Insights	
Diagramming/ Analogy	
Personal Translation	

ENVISIONING THE BIBLE
Colossians 3:1-12; Romans 12:1,2

Envisioning the Bible presses the Scripture through your soul and spirit in that it causes the core of your person to see your acting, reacting, and speaking in a completely different way. Scientists suggest that we cannot do something that we cannot pre-see ourself doing. This is why Jesus and many of the apostles in Scripture ask us to put on a heart of compassion, be salt and light, and desire the pure milk of the Word when we clearly are not these things. God calls us to pre-see ourselves acting in ways that are not natural for us at present. We are to pre-see ourselves acting righteously, then act in those ways in the real world until it is our natural instinct to act this way.

One of the clearest examples of this process of picturing our self living out what we do not possess is in Colossians 3:1-12. Look at the specific places where God, through the Apostle Paul, tells us to picture something as true for us or act in a way that is not yet reality.

> *Therefore if you have been raised up with Christ, <u>keep seeking the things above</u>, where Christ is, seated at the right hand of God. <u>Set your mind on the things above</u>, not on the things that are on earth. For you have died and your life is hidden with Christ*

in God. When Christ, who is our life, is revealed, then you also will be revealed with Him in glory. Therefore <u>consider the members of your earthly body as dead to immorality, impurity, passion, evil desire, and greed</u>, which amounts to idolatry. For it is because of these things that the wrath of God will come upon the sons of disobedience, and in them you also once walked, when you were living in them. But now you also, put them all aside: anger, wrath, malice, slander, and abusive speech from your mouth. Do not lie to one another, since you laid aside the old self with its evil practices, and have put on the new self who is being renewed to a true knowledge according to the image of the One who created him— a renewal in which there is no distinction between Greek and Jew, circumcised and uncircumcised, barbarian, Scythian, slave and freeman, but Christ is all, and in all. So, as those who have been chosen of God, holy and beloved, <u>put on a heart of compassion, kindness, humility, gentleness and patience; bearing with one another, and forgiving each other</u>, whoever has a complaint against anyone; just as the Lord forgave you, so also should you. <u>Beyond all these things put on love, which is the perfect bond of unity. Let the peace of Christ rule in your hearts</u>, to which indeed you were called in one body; and be thankful.

In a sense we are trying to reprogram ourselves to think, act, speak, and emote in biblical ways. We need to push the God-honoring way of living into our minds, will, emotions, and spirit until we actually do behave like this.

There are two classic ways of envisioning the Bible. First, is where you actually picture the Bible stories playing themselves out in your head. You see the characters. You mentally use your five senses to make the Bible story come to life inside your head. You hear them speak. You smell the dusty roads, the aroma of the incense, etc. You touch the hem of the garment, the hide of the animal as it passes. You carry the poles of the ark as it is carried into the Jordan. You feel the dirt splashed with Jesus' spit as he stirs it before it is rubbed on the eyes of the man born blind. You see Jesus growing taller as He begins to rise above the crowd and into heaven. You see the bloody head of John the Baptist presented to Herod Antipas as a present.

The second way of envisioning the Bible is where you see yourself actually living out the Bible in a way that is not currently true of you at present. You speak out affirmations of biblical truth that you are asking God to make a normal part of your life within a few days, weeks, or months. You actually picture yourself going through your day tomorrow doing the biblically right thing instead of your typical way of acting or speaking. You picture yourself three years from now being much more of what God wants you to be, how you will be acting, what your relationships will be like, and what your life will be like when you allow God's truth to be your normal pattern of action.

The greatest force for change, the scientists tell us, is visualizing your goals already achieved in the future. When that is coupled with the power of God's Word, the combination is unbeatable. When you picture your life being everything God wants it to be three years from now, you activate your mind, your emotions, your will, and most importantly the power of God to allow you to become what only God can transform you into.

Envisioning the Bible is a way of pressing the Bible through our mind. It forces our minds eye to "see" the Bible. If the Bible and our understanding of the Bible remain an abstract concept, then we will not be impacted by the Bible.

One of the ways that this technique of biblical visualization has changed my life is to visualize Mark 12:30,31 as true in my life.

Mark 12:30,31: "You shall love the Lord your God with all your heart, soul, mind and strength and your neighbor as yourself."

> What would it look like if I were really loving God with all my heart, all my soul, all my might?
>> When I drove the freeway?
>> When I was at home?
>> When I was at work?
>> When I was talking with my kids?
>> When I was at church?
>> When I was enjoying the weekend?
>
> What would it look like if I were loving my wife, my children, my friends, my colleagues, bosses and subordinates as I loved myself?
>> When I drove the freeway?
>> When I was at home?
>> When I was at work?
>> When I was talking with my kids?
>> When I was at church?
>> When I was enjoying the weekend?
>
> What would it look like if I were really righteously loving myself?
>> When I drove the freeway?
>> When I was at home?
>> When I was at work?
>> When I was talking with my kids?
>> When I was at church?
>> When I was enjoying the weekend?

I began picturing five years in the future and myself actually living out these verses. I began asking for God for the time, money, qualities, home, friends, health, etc. to make that vision take place.

What is amazing is that I wrote down almost impossible things that would have to be true if I were to be living out that verse at the next level and God is answering those prayers. It is astounding. He wants us to live out His commands.

I can remember when my youth pastor used to make me pre-see my dates based upon biblical passages about purity; such as, 1 Thessalonians 4:1-3. He would make me tell him what I was going to say when I picked her up. What I was going to say to her father. What I was going to do when we went to dinner and the movies.

He always focused on what I was going to do based upon a particular verse; not what I was not going to do. He wanted me to pre-see what I was going to do. He even had me pre-see the end of the date. He made me pre-see ending the date righteously instead of immorally. What is amazing is that what I pre-saw is what happened. I ended up doing what I had seen myself do.

I can remember when I had a date with a young woman who was very willing to get into heavy petting and the like, but my youth pastor's work at pre-seeing of what I would do based upon various Scriptures allowed me to not get sucked into the immorality that was certainly available. I saw my youth pastor right after that date, and I was so excited about how the power of the Scriptures had allowed me to act totally different than my internal impulses.

Just like athletes pictures themselves going through their athletic performance perfectly from beginning to end, so you should picture yourself going through some aspect of your life in a perfectly Christ-like way. See each step of the process executed by you perfectly. You must be able to see yourself living out the Christ-like way before you will ever actually do it in your actual life. Once you lock on to a place where God wants you to change, think through what doing it perfectly right would look like. Go over this and over this mental movie until you are clear what you do, what you say, what your attitude is, and so on. Then try this new way in your actual encounters with people.

Do this pre-seeing in one area of your life that needs changing. Do not try and change everything at once but work on one area at a time and pre-see yourself acting completely biblically Christ-like. It will be strange to act in this new way at first, but it will eventually become your preferred mode. It will also draw the blessing of God to that area of your life where it has not been previously:

> Greeting your colleagues
> Meeting with a client
> Meeting with an enemy
> Going to church
> Driving the freeway
> Coming home from work or school
> Resisting the temptations of drugs, sex, stealing
> Speaking kindly and helpfully to parents or boss
> Interacting with our spouse with joy, peace, and patience
> Taking time with children or parents

We all know that we should behave and speak differently than we do in certain situations and relationships. This will never change just by wishing it would. We must meditate on the biblical ideas and what they would look like in our life with us doing them. Colossians 3:12 tells us that we must put on a heart of compassion. It is not something we feel like. It is a put on job. It is something we do because we want the love of Christ to flow through us. We are acting like Christ even though at the beginning we do not actually feel like acting in this way. We know that this is what God wants, and so we cooperate with God before we actually feel like it. The grace of God will move through our bodies and energize us to be more Christ-like.

This is not a quick mental brush through these events. It is a painstaking mental movie of a new you acting Christ-like in these various segments of your life. Where ever you need to act different, you need to see yourself acting in this different biblical way. See yourself over and over acting differently, and you will begin to act that way.

You must actually picture yourself going through your day tomorrow doing the biblically right thing instead of your typical way of acting or speaking. You picture yourself three years from now being much more of what God wants you to be, how you will be acting, what your relationships will be like, and what your life will be like when you allow God's truth to be your normal pattern of action.

I have included a number of Biblical Meditation and prayer exercises here because this is so crucial to becoming fully alive in Christ. Remember, if you cannot see yourself acting Christian before it happens, then you won't be able to act Christian when it happens.

	Date: _____
Scripture	
Slow Repetition	
Memorization	
Study	
Singing	
Confessing	
Praying	
Envisioning	
Personalize	
Journal Insights	
Diagramming/ Analogy	
Personal Translation	

	Date: _____
Scripture	
Slow Repetition	
Memorization	
Study	
Singing	
Confessing	
Praying	
Envisioning	
Personalize	
Journal Insights	
Diagramming/ Analogy	
Personal Translation	

Biblical Meditation and Prayer Exercise

One of the classic ways of envisioning the Scriptures is to use the lists of commands in the Scriptures and to write down or speak out what your life would be like if you lived out these truths of Christ-likeness.

If I really loved God with all my heart I would…
If I really loved myself as I should I would…
If I really tried to fill my marriage with love I would…
If I really loved my children/parents as Christ would want then I would…
If I really worked for God then I would… at my job.
If I were really interested in deep Christian fellowship then I would…
If I really handled my money the way God wanted me to then I would…
If I were a true Christian friend then I would…
If I were truly salt and light in my community then I would…

Look at each one of these sections and the verses that follow them and finish the sentences that are incomplete here.

Repeat one category of these verses out loud one to five times per day for a week. Let me suggest the following times:

When you get up
When you have breakfast
When you eat lunch
When you eat dinner
When you go to bed at night

Then picture what it would look like for you to actually be doing what the verse says. Mentally see yourself being Christ-like. This cannot be abstract. You have to actually see yourself speaking and doing what the verse says. If you cannot picture what a Christ-like person behaves like, then you cannot act Christian in that area. It needs to be a concrete-clear picture.

Various ideas and changes will come to your mind right after you say these verses. Write down what comes to your mind. These are ideas from God and your own mind of how to make these verses true for you. This is exciting stuff. When you start trying the ideas that come to your mind, there will be more. This starts a chain of positive change that you want to be active in your life.

I have listed verses for each of the ten major relationships of life that tell us how to behave as Christ-followers in that relationship. Pick one of the relationships and envision living what the Scripture says in that relationship of your life. You may also choose to work through each of the relationships one at a time.

God

Mark 12:30
You shall love the Lord your God with all your heart, and with all your soul, and with all your mind, and with all your strength.

Self

Mark 12:31
You shall love your neighbor as yourself.

Matthew 6:33
But seek first His kingdom and His righteousness, and all these things will be added to you.

Ecclesiastes 11:9,10
Rejoice, young man, during your childhood, and let your heart be pleasant during the days of young manhood. And follow the impulses of your heart and the desires of your eyes. Yet know that God will bring you to judgment for all these things. So, remove grief and anger from your heart and put away pain from your body, because childhood and the prime of life are fleeting.

Marriage
Ecclesiastes 9:9
Enjoy life with the woman whom you love all the days of your fleeting life which He has given to you under the sun; for this is your reward in life and in your toil in which you have labored under the sun.

Ephesians 5:25
Husband's love your wives as Christ loved the church.

Ephesians 5:22
Wives adapt yourself to your own husbands, as to the Lord.

Parenting/Family
Ephesians 6:4
Fathers, do not provoke your children to anger, but bring them up in the discipline and instruction of the Lord.

Work
Ephesians 6:5-7
Be obedient to those who are your masters according to the flesh, with fear and trembling, in the sincerity of your heart, as to Christ; not by way of eye-service, as men-pleasers, but as slaves of Christ, doing the will of God from the heart. With good will render service, as to the Lord, and not to men...

Church
Hebrews 10:24,25
Let us consider how to stimulate one another to love and good deeds, not forsaking our own assembling together, as is the habit of some, but encouraging one another; and all the more as you see the day drawing near.

John 13:34,25
A new commandment I give to you, that you love one another, even as I have loved you, that you also love one another. By this all men will know that you are My disciples, if you have love for one another.

Money
Matthew 6:24
No one can serve two masters; for either he will hate the one and love the other, or he will be devoted to one and despise the other. You cannot serve God and wealth.

1 Timothy 6:17
Instruct those who are rich in this present world not to be conceited or to fix their hope on the uncertainty

of riches, but on God, who richly supplies us with all things to enjoy.

Friends

Proverbs 17:17
A friend loves at all times, and a brother is born for adversity.

John 15:13
Greater love has no one than this, that one lay down his life for his friends.

Society

Matthew 5:13-16
You are the salt of the earth; but if the salt has become tasteless, how can it be made salty again? It is no longer good for anything, except to be thrown out and trampled underfoot by men. You are the light of the world. A city set on a hill cannot be hidden; nor does anyone light a lamp and put it under a basket, but on the lampstand, and it gives light to all who are in the house. Let your light shine before men in such a way that they may see your good works, and glorify your Father who is in heaven.

Enemies

Matthew 5:42-25
You have heard that it was said, 'YOU SHALL LOVE YOUR NEIGHBOR and hate your enemy.' But I say to you, love your enemies and pray for those who persecute you, so that you may be sons of your Father who is in heaven; for He causes His sun to rise on the evil and the good, and sends rain on the righteous and the unrighteous.

Luke 6:31-37

Treat others the same way you want them to treat you. If you love those who love you, what credit is that to you? For even sinners love those who love them. If you do good to those who do good to you, what credit is that to you? For even sinners do the same. If you lend to those from whom you expect to receive, what credit is that to you? Even sinners lend to sinners in order to receive back the same amount. But love your enemies, and do good, and lend, expecting nothing in return; and your reward will be great, and you will be sons of the Most High; for He Himself is kind to ungrateful and evil men. Be merciful, just as your Father is merciful.

	Date: _____
Scripture	
Slow Repetition	
Memorization	
Study	
Singing	
Confessing	
Praying	
Envisioning	
Personalize	
Journal Insights	
Diagramming/ Analogy	
Personal Translation	

Biblical Meditation and Prayer Exercise

Another way to envision Scripture is to see yourself doing the ideas and principles of Scripture. This can be done through mental picturing and through affirmations of your already being what God wants. You will begin to live up to and into the affirmations you make about yourself. There is something powerful when you affirm out loud what you want to be by the grace of God even though you are not yet those things.

The following are affirmations in this direction. I would suggest that you say one of the following affirmations one to five times a day for a week and watch yourself grow into these truths and lifestyles of Christ-likeness. Pick one relationship in your life and say these affirmations five times a day for a week or longer. Watch the change happen.

The Fruit of the Spirit

Love: I am alert every day to God's impulses to meet some one's needs, to pursue their soul, and/or to please others in some way.

Joy: I am sensitive to the prompting of God to deepen my relationships and be positive with others.

Peace: I stop making war needlessly with others and find a way to be in harmony with others if possible.

Patience: I constantly draw upon God's power to keep persevering toward a righteous goal.

Kindness: I am alert to how I can adjust my interactions to be more pleasant, merciful, and encouraging.

Goodness: I listen hard for God's specific ways of benefiting others.

Meekness: I am flexible and calm when my expectations are not met, and I make thoughtful requests and wise adaptations.

Faithfulness: I am alert to the Lord's promptings to trust Him and stay the righteous course.

Self-Control: I am sensitive to the Holy Spirit as He seeks to moderate my desires.

Against such things there is no law

	Date: _____
Scripture	
Slow Repetition	
Memorization	
Study	
Singing	
Confessing	
Praying	
Envisioning	
Personalize	
Journal Insights	
Diagramming/ Analogy	
Personal Translation	

Beatitudes

Blessed are the poor in spirit for theirs is the kingdom of heaven: I am aware of how I need God and the others. I am teachable, and I do not need to be the center of attention.

Blessed are those who mourn for they shall be comforted: I take the time to grieve the losses and pain in my life, and I do not make excuses or cover up my failures and shortcomings.

Blessed are the meek for they shall inherit the earth: I am flexible and calm when my expectations are not met, and I make thoughtful requests and wise adaptations.

Blessed are those who hunger and thirst after righteousness for they shall be satisfied: I have a burning desire to see the right things done, and I know the righteous cause(s) God wants me to promote.

Blessed are the merciful for they shall receive mercy: I forgive and look for second-mile opportunities to overcome feelings of vengeance.

Blessed are the pure in heart for they shall see God: I make sure that my core thoughts and images are pure and positive.

Blessed are the peacemakers for they shall be called the sons of God: I help others stop making war with each other and help them live in harmony with each other and God.

Blessed are those who have been persecuted for righteousness for theirs is the kingdom of heaven: I stand up for what is right even if it is inconvenient and costly.

Blessed are you when men revile you and persecute you and say all manner of evil against you falsely on account of Me. Rejoice and be exceedingly glad, for so they persecuted the prophets who were before you: I openly identify with Jesus and some people are offended by that.

	Date: _____
Scripture	
Slow Repetition	
Memorization	
Study	
Singing	
Confessing	
Praying	
Envisioning	
Personalize	
Journal Insights	
Diagramming/ Analogy	
Personal Translation	

	Date:
Scripture	
Slow Repetition	
Memorization	
Study	
Singing	
Confessing	
Praying	
Envisioning	
Personalize	
Journal Insights	
Diagramming/ Analogy	
Personal Translation	

Biblical Meditation and Prayer Exercise

One of the ways to actually envision Scripture is to break down biblical truth into affirmations that we can say about ourselves if we were living out what the Word of God said. Take these affirmations and say them out loud multiple times each day. Watch your own actions begin to change as you affirm that you are already living out these truths. In a way this is setting your mind on the things above where Christ is. Pick a section of your life that needs the most reform or direction from the Lord. Say these Scriptural affirmations multiple times per day for a week and record what happens in your life.

Spirituality

I let God evaluate my life every day and I confess what He points out.

I listen every day for the voice of the Holy Spirit to display the fruit of the Spirit.

I mediate on the Bible each day through slow repetition, personalization, visualization, study, journaling, praying.

I pray to God every day, listening and speaking.

I praise, adore, and give thanks to God daily as an individual and weekly as a part of a church.

I am alert to God's service assignments: the daily ones, the church ones, and the community ones.

I identify with Christ whenever He brings someone to me who ask me about my faith.

I fast, at times, for greater spiritual power.

I rent my body to Jesus to love people I don't love.

I give 10 percent+ of my income as a tithe.

	Date: _____
Scripture	
Slow Repetition	
Memorization	
Study	
Singing	
Confessing	
Praying	
Envisioning	
Personalize	
Journal Insights	
Diagramming/ Analogy	
Personal Translation	

Marriage:

Husband Affirmations

I honor my wife every day by complimenting her, telling her I love her, and interrupting my things to do her things.

I understand my wife every day by listening to what she says and what she doesn't say. I know more about her personality, family patterns, leadership styles, love languages than anyone else.

I give my wife security financially, relationally, emotionally, physically, and spiritually.

I build unity in our family by never letting her be the common enemy and by building a large amount of positive shared experiences.

I foster unity and agreement by working a wise process in decision making and by having preset decisions.

I nurture my wife: spiritually by leading; mentally by intimate regular communication; emotionally by daily and weekly romance; physically by tender touch and affection.

I defend my wife from all mental, verbal, physical, emotional, relational, and spiritual attacks.

	Date: _____
Scripture	_____
	_____
Slow Repetition	_____
	_____
Memorization	_____
	_____
Study	_____
	_____
Singing	_____
	_____
Confessing	_____
	_____
Praying	_____
	_____
Envisioning	_____
	_____
Personalize	_____
	_____
Journal Insights	_____
	_____
Diagramming/ Analogy	_____
	_____
Personal Translation	_____
	_____
	_____
	_____

Marriage:

Wife Affirmations

I give my husband respect, appreciation, and value every day from his frame of reference: accomplishments, avoidances, abilities, temperament, spiritual gifts, and strengths.

I appreciate my husband more than any other person in his life.

I adapt my life to make my husband successful and our marriage work.

I lead domestically to ensure that our home life is a nurturing and well-ordered place.

I pursue intimacy with my husband multiple times per week.

I join my husband in some of his interests weekly, monthly, quarterly, and yearly.

I develop a beautiful soul (appreciative, valuing, forgiving, calm, wise, sympathetic, etc.) that my husband will be drawn to while keeping myself attractive physically to my husband (clothes, hair, makeup, weight, etc.).

I give the gift of focused, engaged listening weekly to my husband regarding his life, struggles, victories, fears, doubts, and dreams.

	Date:
Scripture	
Slow Repetition	
Memorization	
Study	
Singing	
Confessing	
Praying	
Envisioning	
Personalize	
Journal Insights	
Diagramming/ Analogy	
Personal Translation	

Familial:

Respect

I value and appreciate each of my children every day for their strengths, accomplishments, avoidances, and personality.

Relationship

I pursue opportunities to work with, play with, and talk with my children every week.

Our family takes multiple vacations each year.

I spend money to accomplish experience events each week, quarter, and year.

Rules

I live within the rules of our family which are based on respect for the moral law of God, the Ten Commandments.

Responsibility

I apologize when I have offended anyone in my family; when I have messed up and made mistakes.

I do my chores and obligations.

	Date: _____
Scripture	
Slow Repetition	
Memorization	
Study	
Singing	
Confessing	
Praying	
Envisioning	
Personalize	
Journal Insights	
Diagramming/ Analogy	
Personal Translation	

Biblical Success in Life:

I am blessed enjoying deep, satisfying, and abundant relationships in every area of life.

My walk with God is deep, interactive, full of guidance, listening, and meaning.

My soul and spirit have an energized contentment as they express who God made them and my body is healthy.

My relationship with my wife is a constant delight, full of respect, communication, security, and intimacy.

I swell with pride as I enjoy my relationship with each of my children, knowing and celebrating their value, watching them live by God's rules, and seeing them embrace their responsibilities as productive human beings.

I am deeply satisfied by my contribution to God's kingdom and this world through my work, filled with meaning because I am making a difference.

I enjoy a close, caring relationship with a group of Christians that I care about and who care for me. They sustain me and manifest unique aspects of my soul.

Financially, I live in balanced godly abundance -- collecting, giving, and managing it all for God's glory.

I impact the community positively through various acts of love and righteousness.

I celebrate those who have chosen to oppose me directly, by loving them and seeking to have God hold them in check against me.

Envisioning The Bible

	Date: _____
Scripture	
Slow Repetition	
Memorization	
Study	
Singing	
Confessing	
Praying	
Envisioning	
Personalize	
Journal Insights	
Diagramming/ Analogy	
Personal Translation	

Biblical Meditation and Prayer Exercise

Work

I fight slothfulness through hard, smart, and perseverant work. 2 Thessalonians 3:10

I maximize my full God-given potential rather than comparing what others have.

I pursue the dream that God has planted in my heart.

I am a team player.

I work for God no matter where I am employed.

I am ever conscious to please Him.

I respect my bosses, subordinates, and colleagues.

I am focused on my work when I am at work.

I adapt myself to the needs of my employer and my bosses whenever possible.

Envisioning The Bible

	Date: _____
Scripture	
Slow Repetition	
Memorization	
Study	
Singing	
Confessing	
Praying	
Envisioning	
Personalize	
Journal Insights	
Diagramming/ Analogy	
Personal Translation	

Monetary Principles for Living Biblically

I build Godly boundaries around my finances and possessions. Matthew 6:24-27

I love God, myself, and others and I use money to help do it. Mark 12:29-31; 1 Timothy 6:10-11

I realize that all my money comes from my ability to love (to meet real needs).

I stay within God's income range for me. Proverbs 30:7-9

I am building up enough relationships and money so that I can dedicate 100 percent of my time to the Lord at some point in my life.

I refuse immoral, illegal, and unethical income. Proverbs 15:6; 27; 11:29; Psalm 15

I do not make money through usury. Psalm 15

I pay my taxes. Romans 13:8

I focus on reaching my full righteous potential for God's glory; not what others have. Colossians 3:5; Hebrews 13:5; Ephesians 5:5; Exodus 20:17

I make wise purchases.

I aim at glorifying God through righteousness, love, and peace in everything I do. Romans 14:17; Matthew 6:33

I aim at loving God and others within the ten box in everything I do. Mark 12:29-31; Exodus 20:3-21

I have a money plan for each month. Proverbs 27:25-27

I have six month's salary in an emergency fund. Proverbs 27:23,24

I have $10,000 in a savings account.

I save at least ten percent of my income in order to retire and/or serve the Lord full time without the burden of trading time for money.

I give at least ten percent of my income to my local church as a tithe. Matthew 23:23; Malachi 3:10-15

I give at least one percent of my income to individuals and charitable organizations.

I use my money to promote righteousness, peace, and joy in the Holy Spirit.

I live in contented godly abundance.

I love people and use money; not the other way around.

I maximize my ability to produce righteousness, love, and joy through earned income, passive income, business income, and charitable income.

I stay out of unsecured debt.

I am a generous person. 1 Timothy 6:18

I am focused on God in the area of finances not the accumulation of wealth. 1 Timothy 6:17

Envisioning The Bible

	Date: _____
Scripture	_____
	_____
Slow Repetition	_____
	_____
Memorization	_____
	_____
Study	_____
	_____
Singing	_____
	_____
Confessing	_____
	_____
Praying	_____
	_____
Envisioning	_____
	_____
Personalize	_____
	_____
Journal Insights	_____
	_____
Diagramming/ Analogy	_____
	_____
Personal Translation	_____
	_____
	_____

Personalizing the Bible
Psalms

There is a powerful form of listening prayer called personalizing the Scriptures. This is where you insert your name into actual verses of Scripture and you say or write the verse with your name inserted into it. I have watched people actually be overcome by the Word of God doing this exercise of prayer. God is speaking directly to them in the verse. Too often the Scriptures remain a distant ancient text which does not come to life in our soul. This way of praying will change the Scriptures into a powerful life force in you. Say these verses with your name inserted in them right now.

1 John 2:1 *My little child, _____, I write these things to you so that you, _____ ,may not sin, but if you, _____, do sin, we (including _____) have an advocate with the Father, Jesus Christ the righteous.*

Romans 8:1 *There is now no condemnation (for _____) in Christ Jesus.*

Psalm 23 *The Lord is my, _____, shepherd. I, _____, shall not want. He makes me,_____, lie down in green pastures. He leads me, _____ ,beside quiet waters for His name sake.*

Even though I, _____, walk through the valley of the shadow of death I, _____, will fear no evil. His rod and staff they comfort me, _____.

Philippians 1:6 *I am confident that He who began a good work in you, _____ ,will perfect it until the day of Christ Jesus.*

This is one of the most powerful and emotional ways of meditating on the Bible. Take a Scripture verse and insert your name into the verse in the place of every pronoun and in every place where it will make sense to put your name without destroying the flow of Scripture. Your personalization of the Scripture quickly becomes a prayer as you speak to God and listen back to His response. Personalizing the Scripture often leads to a strong emotional connection to God and His words to you.

One of the reasons that so many people find the Psalms so encouraging, comforting, and strengthening is that much of the Psalms are David's personalization of the first five books of Moses. David memorized the first five books of Moses and then pushed those verses through His soul and coupled them with his experience and out came these songs and poems. The Psalms are the expressions of a soul's reaching for God in the midst of turmoil, victory, and pain.

I remember one woman who was led out of a false cult and into the marvelous light of Christ as Savior by personalizing John 3:16. She inserted her name into John 3:16 in three places and saw that what the Bible was talking about was the exact opposite of the legalistic pathway to heaven that this cult was talking about. She just kept saying the verse until she found a church that taught what that verse clearly declared. It took her almost five years to make that transition from cultic member to Christian, but it happened.

John 3:16 *For God so loved _____ that He have His only begotten Son for _____ that if _____ believes in Him _____ shall not perish but _____ have everlasting life.*

Personalizing the Bible is another way of pressing the Bible into and through our emotions. So much of what we do is a product of our emotional reaction to our present world. If our emotions are subconsciously confronted with the Word of God, a different person emerges after the encounter.

As I have worked with men who are struggling with lust and sexual purity, I have found that one of the most powerful Scriptures for them to personalize is Romans 6:1-23. It gives them new power against temptation. The men open their Bibles and begin writing out the text with their name inserted everywhere they can and the sin they are being tempted to do.

> What do you say then, Bill? Are you going to continue lusting so that grace may increase? How stupid, Bill!! How shall you, Bill, who died to lust still live in it? Or do you not know that everyone including you, Bill, who has been baptized into Christ Jesus have been baptized into His death? Consider yourself dead to lusting, Bill. Stop letting lust tell you want to do, Bill. And stop giving lust the parts of your body to use: your mind, your hands, your mouth, your eyes. Bill, stop that. Bill, lust doesn't have to be the master over you with your obeying it's every suggestion. Listen, Bill, if you do what lust wants all the time, then you are the slave of lust; the more you obey its promptings, the more bondage and slavery you will be in. Stop doing what lust wants; do what Christ wants.

One of the most powerful personalized Scriptures that God used in my life is 1 John 2:1-3.

Spend time personalizing a passage of Scripture.

Personalizing The Bible

Scripture	Date: _____
Slow Repetition	
Memorization	
Study	
Singing	
Confessing	
Praying	
Envisioning	
Personalize	
Journal Insights	
Diagramming/ Analogy	
Personal Translation	

	Date: _____
Scripture	
Slow Repetition	
Memorization	
Study	
Singing	
Confessing	
Praying	
Envisioning	
Personalize	
Journal Insights	
Diagramming/ Analogy	
Personal Translation	

	Date:
Scripture	
Slow Repetition	
Memorization	
Study	
Singing	
Confessing	
Praying	
Envisioning	
Personalize	
Journal Insights	
Diagramming/ Analogy	
Personal Translation	

	Date: _____
Scripture	_____
Slow Repetition	_____
Memorization	_____
Study	_____
Singing	_____
Confessing	_____
Praying	_____
Envisioning	_____
Personalize	_____
Journal Insights	_____
Diagramming/ Analogy	_____
Personal Translation	_____

Journaling Your Interactions With The Bible

As you meditatively pray on the Bible, hundreds of ideas will pop into your mind. Some will deal with the Scripture you are meditating on and some will relate to your life. These insights and ideas need to be recorded. The more you pay attention to these insights by writing them down, the more you will get. This is why I suggest you start carrying around a journal notebook so that you can jot down ideas that come to mind. These insights may be like diary entries or they may be word studies or they may be sketches and diagrams. Carrying the journal is a way of saying, "God, I am ready for anything you want to drop into my mind."

I have included pages in the back of this book for you to journal your thoughts, reactions, ideas, and interactions with God. It is often very instructive to look back and see how, over time, God has been saying the same things for a period of weeks or months.

There is also something cathartic about writing down your emotions, struggles, victories, and defeats. This is a way to process the pain in your life out of your body and be released from it. If God were to make an appointment with you, wouldn't you bring a pen and paper to write down what He said? Well He is ready to meet with you through Biblical Meditation.

Many Christians have found that it is helpful to write out their prayers at times. This focuses their thoughts and requests. It keeps their mind from wandering. I have watched numerous people who can pray for an hour or more through the writing of a letter to God. They tell me that they could not pray that long if they had to just speak to God.

In order to try out this form of prayerful Biblical Meditation, begin writing a prayer to the Lord about the Scripture that you have been meditating upon in other ways. Write the letter knowing that He is reading it as you write and that you want to have Him read it later also.

Dear Lord Jesus,
I want to talk with you about my spiritual life because you say in your word (Philippians 2:12-15) that you will help me work out my salvation with fear and trembling. It seems to me that I do not always sense where you are working in me. I also sense that you are working in and on areas that I do not necessarily want you to work on. I know that You are working on my choice in romantic friendships. I am not all that interested in the people that I think I am supposed to be interested in, and I am way too interested in the people who will pull me away from You. Can we talk about that? Isn't there someone who is interesting and godly? How do I cooperate with You to have more of my relationship with You show up in other parts of my life? It seems like my spiritual life is still too distant from the rest of my life.

I would also like to pray for Jim as he is going through difficult times with the loss of his job. Please make Yourself more aware to him. I think he needs to be willing to let You work on his relational skills and humility if he is going to get the job that he really wants and has the skills for.

Can we talk about my work? I do not know what You want me to do at work to show that I am a Christian or that I am different. Everybody seems to be watching to see me mess up so that they can accuse the Christian of being a hypocrite. I want to do better but I am not perfect. You say in this passage that I am a work in progress. I agree with You but no one else seems to want to let me be a work in progress. What are You working on at work in me? What am I missing? I think I am doing pretty well. I hope what you are wanting to work on will help me get a raise.

I have this friend, Jeanie, who is a nice girl but at times I can't stand her. She says that she is a Christian, but I don't see You working in her at all. I have not seen one change since she says that she became a Christian. Can I confront her over this? Can I just get away from her when she is obnoxious and selfish? Do I have to help her work out her salvation or is that between You and her?

Can we talk about the whole money thing and what You want in that area? Do you want me to be poor? I feel like if I give a tithe of my income to the church, then I will be poor and they will be rich. How does salvation work for money? Is it all about giving to the church? Do You have ways you want me to handle my money that I am not doing now? Is it okay to be rich?

I feel like at times you want me to volunteer more to help people, but I don't have lots of time or desire. Could You make it clearer who I am supposed to help? Where and how much?

Thanks for listening,
Christian

	Date:
Scripture	
Slow Repetition	
Memorization	
Study	
Singing	
Confessing	
Praying	
Envisioning	
Personalize	
Journal Insights	
Diagramming/ Analogy	
Personal Translation	

Journaling Your Interactions With The Bible

	Date:
Scripture	
Slow Repetition	
Memorization	
Study	
Singing	
Confessing	
Praying	
Envisioning	
Personalize	
Journal Insights	
Diagramming/ Analogy	
Personal Translation	

DIAGRAM OR ANALOGIZE THE BIBLE

This particular method of Biblical Meditation is most often employed in the Psalms, wisdom literature of the Old Testament, and the stories of Jesus. This is where the Scriptural truth is put in a picture form, schematic, or analogy. This often highlights the truth(s) in new and powerful ways.

I know of a chaplain who finds that if he can diagram a schematic of what this verse is declaring, then he can easily and permanently grasp it. When David was conversing with God, he took the truths from the first five books of Moses and merged them with the rock formations and springs around him. Out of that merger came his descriptions of God as a refuge and fortress, as well as ultimately Jesus' description of Himself as living water.

> Draw a schematic of what this verse is saying.
> Sketch out the results of this verse.
> Diagram the consequences if this verse is ignored.
> The truth or actions of this verse is like…
> The positive results in this verse are like…
> The negative consequences implied by this verse can be compared to…

When I am trying to understand a passage, I know that if I will diagram out what I think God is saying or wants me to do, I can gain clarity on the truth. God has done this, and if I do this then He promises in this verse that He will do this over here.

	Date: _____
Scripture	
Slow Repetition	
Memorization	
Study	
Singing	
Confessing	
Praying	
Envisioning	
Personalize	
Journal Insights	
Diagramming/ Analogy	
Personal Translation	

Diagram Or Analogize The Bible

Scripture	Date: _____
Slow Repetition	
Memorization	
Study	
Singing	
Confessing	
Praying	
Envisioning	
Personalize	
Journal Insights	
Diagramming/ Analogy	
Personal Translation	

Personal Translation of the Bible

One of the unexpectedly insightful ways of impacting your life with the Bible is to write your own personal amplified or simplified translation of the verse or section you have been meditating upon. Even though you have been rutting around in the text for a while, something happens when you put it all together and write it out or say it in your own vernacular version. The Scripture hits you with a new power or a different twist.

The *Living Bible* that has been so helpful to many people in getting into biblical truth is nothing more than one man's personal translation of the Bible. Kenneth Taylor meditated on the Bible and wrote a simplified paraphrase of what the Bible was saying -- for his kids, his wife, and himself. His personal translation does not get the Bible right in every case and sometimes it resembles a commentary on the Bible, but it powerfully impacted him and hundreds of thousands of others over the last fifty years. The same can be said for Eugene Peterson's personal translation of the Bible called *The Message*.

Now don't mistake these personal translations of the Bible for the Bible itself. They are not the Bible. But they do mediate the Bible to us and help us immerse ourselves in the Bible in a deeper way. Now the point of the *Living Bible* or *The Message* paraphrase is not to have you read them, though that is not bad; it is to have you write your own personal paraphrase of the Bible. Do it for your kids and/or your grandkids so that they can be overcome by the power of the Bible. Do it for yourself so that God can speak deep into your soul, in your way, about His truth.

I am amazed at the naiveté and even stupidity that people often believe that Christ would do in certain situations. Would the creator and ruler of the universe always have a syrupy sweet and simplistic answer to every problem? No. Would the ALL WISE God have a Pollyanna solution to the complexities of life? Would the All-knowing God not take into account how other people would react, what they would say, and whether it was in their best interest? Of course He would.

Many of us have retained a third-grade understanding of Jesus that we got from Sunday school; and we have not allowed Christ to be the creator, ruler, and sustainer of everything. Our understanding of God must grow up. This is why it is absolutely essential that we meditate on the biblical material. It and it alone will fill our minds with the true size and wonder of God the Father, God the Son, and God the Holy Spirit.

	Date:
Scripture	
Slow Repetition	
Memorization	
Study	
Singing	
Confessing	
Praying	
Envisioning	
Personalize	
Journal Insights	
Diagramming/ Analogy	
Personal Translation	

Personal Translation Of The Bible

	Date: _____
Scripture	
Slow Repetition	
Memorization	
Study	
Singing	
Confessing	
Praying	
Envisioning	
Personalize	
Journal Insights	
Diagramming/ Analogy	
Personal Translation	

Further Exercises in Biblical Meditation

The process of Biblical Meditation can take many forms, as you can see, but the key idea is to work from biblical material rather than selfish, worldly, or even demonic sources. When we take the time to fill our mind with Scripture, it will begin to control our thoughts, feelings, and actions. This is the foundation for effective prayer. If you fill your mind with Scripture and you are obeying God's command, you can ask whatever you want and it will be done. God wants prayer to work for you. But He wants you to understand the mental framework for it.

I regularly invite people to find the three to five techniques of Biblical Meditation that works for them and keep using them until they no longer help you develop an intimate relationship with God. When one or more tried and true methods of Biblical Meditation stop working, experiment with some new ones and find the channel that God is broadcasting on. The goal is not to be full of biblical knowledge but to have a deep relationship with God the Father, God the Son, and God the Holy Spirit.

The following are suggestions for new directions in your practice of Biblical Meditation:

The book of Psalms
The Commands of Christ

The book of Philippians
The book of James
The book of 1 John

How To Make Prayer Work

	Date: _____
Scripture	_____
Slow Repetition	_____
Memorization	_____
Study	_____
Singing	_____
Confessing	_____
Praying	_____
Envisioning	_____
Personalize	_____
Journal Insights	_____
Diagramming/ Analogy	_____
Personal Translation	_____

Further Exercises In Biblical Meditation

	Date: _____
Scripture	_____
Slow Repetition	_____
Memorization	_____
Study	_____
Singing	_____
Confessing	_____
Praying	_____
Envisioning	_____
Personalize	_____
Journal Insights	_____
Diagramming/ Analogy	_____
Personal Translation	_____

Conclusion
Rockets have just been strapped to your life

There are few things that will be as life transformative as taking the high test rocket fuel of the Scriptures deep in your soul. You will be changed or you will get away from it. My prayer is that you will do more than look at this as another six-week Bible study. Biblical Meditation is one of the key sources of the power for the Christian because God has breathed His life into the Scriptures (2 Timothy 3:16). Some of the methods for Biblical Meditating will really click with you and some will be lifeless and boring. Go with the ones that are encouraging and power producing. This little book is an encouragement to open your heart to the Bible and let it do its work. The Scriptures will not change much if it is applied externally to your life. You need it to be deep inside the way you think and act. It will only become this active ingredient if you meditate upon it.

Prayer that is Scripture-focused and Scripture-driven will change you and the people around you. This is how prayer works. Just as Jesus says, "If you abide in me and my words abide in you, ask whatever you wish and it will be done unto you."

Inject the truth into your veins and watch your life be transformed

Biblical Meditation and Prayer Exercises

Let me give you a starter list I have put together. Put a check mark by the Scripture when you have meditated upon it.

Psa 1:1-3	Phil 1:6	Jam 1:26	1 John 2:15-18
1 John 2:1,2	1 John 3:1-3	Eph 6:1-4	2 Tim 3:16
Col 1:8-10	John 3:16	Col 3:10-12	Ex 20:1-17
Phil 2:1-10	Rom 8:28,29	1 Cor 3:13	2 Cor 10:5
James 1:2-5	1 Thess 4:3-5	Rom 6:1-6	Rom 6:11-16
Gal 5:16	Gal 5:22-25	Col 3:1,2,5,12	2 Pet 1:5-8
Heb 12:1,2	Gen 1:26	Heb 12:4,6,11	Psa 19:14
Matt 28:18-20	Psa 119:9-11	Ex 34:6,7	Rom 11:33
1 Tim 6:15,16	Pro 23:4,5	1 Thess 5:23	Rev 20:11-15
Rev 22:12-14	Rev 21:1,2	Eph 4:11-13	Col 1:9-12
John 14:16,17	Heb 4:14-16	Rev 20:6	2 Cor 5:10

Let me suggest that you take a verse or the whole section from the above list and write out the verse(s) and push through each Biblical Meditation technique on that particular verse. This will drive the truths of that verse deep into your soul and spirit. While the changes will not be evident quickly, the Scripture will begin to change you from the inside out. I have included a separate page on each of the various techniques so that you can see how to progressively go through all the techniques on one particular verse.

It is the pages upon pages of practicing these techniques of Biblical Meditative prayer that God used to chisel many of the rough spots in my character. If we do not use Scripture as our change catalyst, then He has to use the difficulties and trials of our everyday lives. It is better to have the changes He wants begin from the inside and work their way out instead of start from the outside and try and make their way in.

On the left side of these blank pages is a template listing all the various forms of Biblical Meditative prayer. Take the verse or verses and write them out on the first of the blank pages and then spend some time doing each of the techniques on that passage. Each of the pages will have a different technique as you push that particular Scripture through your soul, spirit, and body. The exciting process of filling up a whole book of your wrestling with God will be an amazing legacy to those who follow after you.

You may find that you enjoy one or two of the techniques of Biblical Meditative prayer more than others and want to spend more time using those ways. In this way you may find that you can shorten your processing through the Scripture down to three to five prayerful techniques that work especially well for you. That is fine, but don't forget that there will be times when those other means of Biblical Meditative prayer will unlock greater riches in the Scripture.

Some of you will be helping others with their Christian life and there will be particular verses that will be powerful in the life of those you are helping. Plug these verses into this process and have them pray over these verses in this way and watch God work in deep and long lasting ways. God is alive in His Word if we would just pay enough attention to it.

Feel free to copy these pages and put them in a separate binder or folder to keep your insights and expanding prayer life together.

Conclusion: Rockets Have Just Been Strapped To Your Life

Scripture	Date: _____
Slow Repetition	
Memorization	
Study	
Singing	
Confessing	
Praying	
Envisioning	
Personalize	
Journal Insights	
Diagramming/ Analogy	
Personal Translation	

	Date: _____
Scripture	
Slow Repetition	
Memorization	
Study	
Singing	
Confessing	
Praying	
Envisioning	
Personalize	
Journal Insights	
Diagramming/ Analogy	
Personal Translation	

Conclusion: Rockets Have Just Been Strapped To Your Life

Scripture	Date: _____
Slow Repetition	
Memorization	
Study	
Singing	
Confessing	
Praying	
Envisioning	
Personalize	
Journal Insights	
Diagramming/ Analogy	
Personal Translation	

How To Make Prayer Work

Scripture	Date: _____
Slow Repetition	
Memorization	
Study	
Singing	
Confessing	
Praying	
Envisioning	
Personalize	
Journal Insights	
Diagramming/ Analogy	
Personal Translation	

	Date: _____
Scripture	
Slow Repetition	
Memorization	
Study	
Singing	
Confessing	
Praying	
Envisioning	
Personalize	
Journal Insights	
Diagramming/ Analogy	
Personal Translation	

	Date: _____
Scripture	
Slow Repetition	
Memorization	
Study	
Singing	
Confessing	
Praying	
Envisioning	
Personalize	
Journal Insights	
Diagramming/ Analogy	
Personal Translation	

Conclusion: Rockets Have Just Been Strapped To Your Life

Date: _____

Scripture	_____
Slow Repetition	_____
Memorization	_____
Study	_____
Singing	_____
Confessing	_____
Praying	_____
Envisioning	_____
Personalize	_____
Journal Insights	_____
Diagramming/ Analogy	_____
Personal Translation	_____

	Date:
Scripture	
Slow Repetition	
Memorization	
Study	
Singing	
Confessing	
Praying	
Envisioning	
Personalize	
Journal Insights	
Diagramming/ Analogy	
Personal Translation	

Conclusion: Rockets Have Just Been Strapped To Your Life

	Date: _____
Scripture	_____
Slow Repetition	_____
Memorization	_____
Study	_____
Singing	_____
Confessing	_____
Praying	_____
Envisioning	_____
Personalize	_____
Journal Insights	_____
Diagramming/ Analogy	_____
Personal Translation	_____

How To Make Prayer Work

	Date:
Scripture	
Slow Repetition	
Memorization	
Study	
Singing	
Confessing	
Praying	
Envisioning	
Personalize	
Journal Insights	
Diagramming/ Analogy	
Personal Translation	

Conclusion: Rockets Have Just Been Strapped To Your Life

Scripture	Date: _____
Slow Repetition	_____
Memorization	_____
Study	_____
Singing	_____
Confessing	_____
Praying	_____
Envisioning	_____
Personalize	_____
Journal Insights	_____
Diagramming/ Analogy	_____
Personal Translation	_____

APPENDIX #1 BIBLE STUDY

(Excerpt from the chapter on Bible Study in "Spiritual Disciplines of a C.H.R.I.S.T.I.A.N." by Gil Stieglitz)

THE DISCIPLINES OF INTERACTION: BIBLE STUDY

Mike's face glowed with excitement and anticipation. "I am a totally different person today than I was six weeks ago. I cannot believe the change. Everybody is beginning to notice that I really am a different person. I would not have believed that it was possible if you had told me. These simple little spiritual exercises have put me in a totally different place after only six weeks. Everything about my life is now different. It is amazing!!!"

Many years later, Mike let me know that one of the incredible side benefits of learning the discipline of Bible study has been that his spiritual life is not dependent upon the pastor at his church. He said, "I walk with God every day because I know how to hear Him speak to me from His Word." Too many Christians are weak and unable to live out the Christian life. The disciplines of Bible study and prayer will energize and direct the believer into the Christ-like life and into intimacy with God.

Many people desperately want God to speak to them. What they don't realize is that He has already spoken to them in a living book called the Bible, both Old and New Testaments. When a Christian learns how to study the Bible, he is accessing God's words and can actually hear the voice of God (Hebrews 4:12). When the words of Scripture are studied and embraced, the voice of God speaks to the waiting listener. In order to have a dialogue with God, we must talk to God (prayer) and hear from God (Bible study).

The Bible itself instructs the believer to dig deep into the spiritual nutrients in the Word of God (2 Timothy 2:15). There is spiritual meat waiting for those who hunt for the depth of the text of Scripture. The techniques of in-depth Bible study are not complicated, but the results are deeply transformational. In the years that I spent teaching people how to walk with God, the spiritual discipline of Bible study has proven to be one of the most transformational of all the disciplines. Listen to what the Bible says about the power of Bible study:

"Be diligent to present yourself approved to God as a workman who does not need to be ashamed, handling accurately the word of truth." 2 Timothy 2:15

"All Scripture is inspired by God and profitable for teaching, for reproof, for correction, for training in righteousness; that the man of God may be adequate, equipped for every good work." 2 Timothy 3:16,17

"How can a young man keep his way pure? By keeping it according to Thy word. With all my heart I have sought Thee; Do not let me wander from Thy commandments." Psalm 119:9-10

In his book, *The Celebration of Discipline*, Richard Foster helps us see the value of disciplined Bible study.

"The purpose of the Spiritual Disciplines is the total transformation of the person. It aims at replacing old destructive habits of thought with new life-giving habits. Nowhere is this purpose more clearly seen than in the Discipline of study. The apostle Paul tells us that the way we are transformed is through the renewal of the mind (Romans 12:2). The mind is renewed by applying it to those things that will transform it. 'Finally, brethren, whatever is true, whatever is honorable, whatever is just, whatever is pure, whatever is lovely, whatever is gracious, if there is anything worthy of praise, think about these things' (Philippians 4:8). The Discipline of Study is the primary vehicle to bring us to 'think about these things.' Therefore, we should rejoice that we are not left to our own devices but have been given this means of God's grace for the changing of our inner spirit." (Foster, Richard. *"Celebration of Discipline,"* Harper & Row Publishers, New York. 1978. p 54)

Very few things can prepare a person for the exhilaration of hearing God speak directly from His inspired Word. It is as though a verse of Scripture lifts off the page and begins to call out to the anxious believer, "Study me; I have a message from God for you." Paying close attention to the Scripture, which is the essence of Bible study, is like leaning in to hear the whispered comments of God.

Preparation for Bible Study

It is helpful to have a period of prayer and worship before beginning Bible study. The warm-up period is to put the heart in the right place for an audience with the Almighty. Some people play worship music or work through a time of prayer. If the pressures of your life are keeping you from focusing on the Lord, then the warm-up time may need to be longer. This warm-up period does not have to be long; many times a short anticipatory prayer and then a leap into the deep end of Scripture is exhilarating. The anticipation that God will speak through the study of His Word is often too enticing to put off for long.

Overview of the Three Parts of Bible Study

Studying the Bible is not complicated or reserved for the professional. In fact, when Christians are taught how to study the Bible it usually unleashes them to move in new directions and with power that they did not possess before. This next section on the three steps of Bible study is crucial to the development of the Christian life. Whole books that detail the process of Bible study are excellent resources for the growing Christian: *The Joy of Discovery Bible Study*, by Oletta Wald; *Dynamic Bible Study Methods*, by Rick Warren; *Living by the Book*, by Howard Hendricks.

"The process of studying the Bible involves three steps: **Observation, Interpretation, and Application.** These three steps allow God to speak personally to us out of His inspired Word. Rick Warren put it this way in his excellent book, *Dynamic Bible Study Methods*, "For many years every time I heard a good sermon or some in-depth Bible teaching, I would leave the meeting frustrated, wondering to myself, 'How did he find all of that in this text?' I wanted to be able to discover those truths on my own. In addition, I often felt guilty because people were always telling me I ought to study the Bible, but when I tried to study it, I didn't know what to do. So I would get discouraged and give up. Since those days of frustration, I have discovered that most Christians sincerely want to study their Bibles on their own, but they just don't know how..." (Warren, Rick. *Dynamic Bible Study Methods*, Victor Books, Wheaton, IL. 1989 p 53)

People are awestruck and deeply touched by God through studying His Word. When a person sits down to honestly study God's Word, with the anticipation that God will speak out of His Word, that person will not be disappointed. God is more willing to speak directly to us than we are willing to listen.

Observation

The observation phase of Bible study is nothing more than taking careful notice of a passage of Scripture. The Bible is the inspired and inerrant word of God and paying attention to its details allows for a deeper connection to the Author of this Living Book and to the truth in it. There are four basic ways of paying close attention to the Scriptures: reading, asking questions, circling key words, and diagramming. Each of these is a way to observe the passage and appreciate its richness. The Bible is a collection of God- breathed writings of different types: poetry, songs, teaching, narrative, proverbs, history, letters, etc. While each form of literature is different, these basic techniques work across the types of material. Look at these four basic techniques for taking careful notice. Once a passage, verse, or chapter of Scripture has been selected, use the four tools to crack open the richness waiting inside.

Reading:
Read three times through the portion of Scripture that you have selected. As you are reading and becoming familiar with this passage, start circling key words, key transitions, major ideas in the passage and anything of interest or note. Write down any questions (factual, conceptual, theological, philosophical, or practical) that come to mind as you read through the passage. Do not try to answer the individual questions at this point but just notice the nuances and possible directions of the text. The better a person is at noticing the subtleties of a passage, the greater the opportunity to hear the voice of God in the ways that He would like to inform and direct a Christian.

Let's use Matthew 4:4 as an example:

Reading #1: Matthew 4:4: "But He answered and said, 'It is written, "MAN SHALL NOT LIVE ON BREAD ALONE, BUT ON EVERY WORD THAT PROCEEDS OUT OF THE MOUTH OF GOD.""''

Reading #2: Matthew 4:4: "**But** He answered and said, 'It is **written**, "**MAN** SHALL NOT **LIVE** ON BREAD **ALONE**, BUT ON **EVERY WORD** THAT PROCEEDS OUT OF THE MOUTH OF GOD.""''

Reading #3: Matthew 4:4: "**But** He *answered* and said, 'It is **written**, "**MAN** SHALL NOT **LIVE** ON *BREAD ALONE*, BUT ON **EVERY WORD** THAT *PROCEEDS* OUT OF THE *MOUTH* OF *GOD.*""''

Diagram: Visually show how each word is connected to the whole.
After having read through the passage and its surrounding context three times, the general shape and ideas of this text will be in your mind. Begin a written diagram of the passage, writing down every word of the text on a separate piece of paper. Diagramming is a process of recording the words of Scripture in a visual way to bring out their connections and importance. Some people who diagram use the formal diagramming method of grammatical construction. Others transfer the words of Scripture into a visual impact in a more free-form approach using the size of the words, brackets, arrows, different color pens, etc., to draw out the meaning of the text. There is something unique and powerful that happens when the believer begins to actually manipulate the words of Scripture visually.

Circle Key Words: mark the key or unknown words.

Once the whole passage or verse is written out before you, then you can begin to circle the key words. Specific words could be key because they seem crucial to understanding the passage either because they mark an important transition within the verse or because you do not know what they mean. Compare other translations of this passage or verse if possible. The different words and phrases that other translators used can be helpful in digging out the true meaning of the text. Write these alternative words or renderings above these key words. It is very helpful to see the key words circled in order to be given a road map into the deep treasures of a passage.

Ask Questions: Ask every conceivable question about a particular passage.

This is where all types of questions are focused on the passage. These are the questions that surface when the initial reading of the passage is done; but then the questioning crawls over every word, phrase, and thought in the passage. These questions would include who, what, where, why, how, and when about every subject and/or concept within the text. Many questions will never be answered or don't need to be answered. Looking at each word, phrase, and thought in the passage and asking the questions focuses the mind on the life-giving words of God.

Interpretation

The interpretation phase of Bible study seeks to determine the meaning of the Scripture. There is only one interpretation, although there can be many different applications of that one truth in the Scriptures to the lives of believers. Correct application can only flow out of correct interpretation. What does the passage mean? What did it mean to those who read it when it was new? Most importantly, what did it mean to the person who authored it?

Define Words: Define the words used in the Scripture.

The first technique for determining meaning is to define the words that appear in the text. Take an English dictionary and begin looking up the words from the verse you are studying. You can also use a Greek or Hebrew dictionary to trace the words back to their original meaning. Write the definition next to the key word or at the bottom

Check Cross References: Look up the other places in the Bible where this subject appears.

One of the best commentators on the Bible is the Bible itself. When you compare what other verses say about a similar subject or idea, it becomes much easier to understand what God is talking about. Many Bibles, computer programs, and separate books give numerous cross references for every verse in the Bible. Look up a few of these cross references for each key idea or key word in your verse or passage. Write out the verses that significantly clarify the verse you are studying.

Check Background Information: Cultural, historical, and archeological information.

Each verse of Scripture was recorded in a specific historical and cultural perspective. The understanding of a verse can be significantly enhanced if one understands this background information. Again, study helps are available in many Bibles, computer programs, and online resources.

Look in Commentaries: Check with respected commentators for their observations, interpretations, and applications of the passage you are studying. See if you have come up with something that no one else has ever seen in a passage. If you have developed an interpretation that no one else has ever seen, then most likely it is wrong. In fact, it is the arrogance of completely new Bible interpretation that is the beginning of almost every cult.

Write Translation: Write your own translation using the expanded definitions and ideas.

Application: What Does God Want Me to Know, Feel, Do?

This is the most exciting part of the spiritual discipline of Bible study. Application is seeking God's face about precisely what He wants to change in your life. The applications are of three different varieties: know, feel, do. Knowledge application changes the way a person thinks. Emotional application changes the way a person feels. Action application changes what a person does.

The following are some of the Know, Feel, and Do application that are possible from the Matthew 4:4 passage:

Know Applications:

Satan will try to tempt me to provide for myself before God provides.

Satan will try to tempt me to use my own power and energy to provide for myself outside of what God has directed me to do.

Quoting Scripture is the best way to stop a Satanic temptation.

I cannot have a fully-orbed life without memorizing, meditating, and studying God's word.

The words of the Bible produce fully-orbed quality of life in those who live them out.

In the same way that I take food in, I must take in the Words of God and do them.

Otherwise I will think thoughts or have ideas that come from the enemy of my soul.

Feel Applications:

God has provided and will provide all I need for physical life and a fully-orbed life.

I do not need to give into the devil or fear his approach for my God has given me weapons: Scripture.

Satan wants to make me feel that God will not provide and that I must impulsively provide for myself because God won't come through.

If God has not provided for something that you think you need, then you don't need it or you are out of the will of God, and He will not provide it for you when you remain where you are. God always provides.

I need to "feel" the power and treasure that is in the Word of God. It is energy for Life.

Do Applications:

I need to memorize Scripture: one a day or one a week. If I don't, I will rob myself of a better quality of existence.

I need to study Scripture every day.

I need to meditate on Scripture through my day.

I need to quote Scripture when I am being tempted to do what I know is wrong.

I need to do a new action that is based on Scripture every day so I can live the full-orbed life.

Every day I eat physical food; I also need to take in the Scriptures or I will not enjoy life to the fullest.

I need to study the Old Testament book of Deuteronomy because Jesus quotes from it in rebuffing each of Satan's attacks.

How Do I do What God Is Asking?

A part of each Bible study is applying it. Application helps us to gain clarity on what God is asking us to do through the Scripture. Application should be very specific. Until application of the study is accomplished, little will change in my life. I must define the action steps that are required to take advantage of the truth of Scripture.

Why Do I Need This Truth Today?

Since God knew that I would be studying this passage today, is there any special significance to what is in the passage for me today? Is this a truth, feeling, or action that I need to add or subtract because it will have long-term benefit for me? As I pray about this day, are there any promptings or warnings to me from God's Spirit about this verse? What is the reason that God wants me to study this verse?

APPENDIX #2 BIBLICAL MEDITATION

(Excerpt from the chapter on Meditation in "Spiritual Disciplines of a C.H.R.I.S.T.I.A.N." by Gil Stieglitz)

THE DISCIPLINES OF REPETITION: BIBLICAL MEDITATION

People are talking about meditation these days as though it were the sole property of the eastern religions. Eastern religions practice a form of meditation. Using broad general categories, there are two types of meditation: **Emptying forms** of meditation and **Content-based forms** of meditation. All meditation is the focused attention of the mind upon something. In emptying forms of meditation the mind is focused on a nonsense idea, word, phrase, or a logical absurdity in order to attempt an escape from the present space-time logical constraints. In content-based meditation the mind is focused on some form of content. There are three forms of content-based meditation: materialistic, spiritual, and biblical. Biblical Meditation is "content-based" meditation with biblical words, ideas, phrases, and precepts as the meditated content. The new biblical qualities, reactions, and ideas will become a part of the person who is being shaped into Christ-likeness. The goal of the Christian is to have the Lord's thoughts become their thoughts (Isaiah 55:6-8, Psalm 1:1-3; Colossians 3:16; Joshua 1:8; Philippians 4:8; Deuteronomy 6:6-9).

The Incredible Power of Biblical Meditation

The most powerful form of transformational life-change known to man is meditation. In fact no long-term life-change can take place without this meditation. The tragedy in Christian circles is that this powerful method is often unknown, unused, and in some cases even reviled. Biblical meditation was common practice in the

Christian church for 1900 years. Yet in the last 150 years biblical meditation has been left behind in the modern church as it searches for newer programs and crowd-pleasing techniques. The prophet Amos tells of a time when there will be a famine in the land, "not a famine for bread, nor a thirst for water, but rather for hearing the words of the Lord." (Amos 8:11) We are living out a fulfillment of that vision. More Bibles are printed than ever before and yet the power of the Bible is not connecting with the souls of God's people. All the power people want for transformational life-change is near but remains untapped.

What is Biblical Meditation?

The idea behind Biblical Meditation is taken from a sheep or cow chewing its cud. The animal chews the grass and works it into a mush and then swallows it. It then brings it back up later to chew it some more. It repeats this process until all the nutrients have been extracted from the grass. Meditation is murmuring or repeating the concepts, ideas, and words of Scripture to extract all the richness and wisdom.

Biblical meditation is referred to in a number of ways in the Scriptures: delighting in Scripture (Psalm 119:16, 34, 47, 70); delighting in the Lord (Psalm 37:4); letting the Word of God richly dwell in your soul (Colossians 3:16); setting your mind on things above (Colossians 3:1); setting your mind on the Spirit (Romans 8:6); renewing your mind (Romans 12:2).

What Are the Techniques of Biblical Meditation?

Down through the centuries of Judeo-Christian history, strong believers have discovered a number of methods for "chewing" Scripture. These techniques move the believer significantly forward in their pursuit of God and attainment of Christ-like living. The following list is not meant to be exhaustive or prioritized. Some will find certain techniques more helpful than others.

Confessionalize Scripture

To confessionalize Scripture is to take the Bible through your will. It is the process of comparing your life with the biblical standard and asking God whether this is true of your life. Every phrase or sentence of Scripture forms a way of examining your life. **First,** each truth or action exposed in that Scripture is confessed as true and important. "Dear Lord, I agree with you that Christians should love one another." **Second,** each truth or action is confessed as something you are doing or something that you are not doing. "Dear Lord, I freely admit that I am having a very difficult time loving this person right now. I know that I should, but I do not. Create in me a heart of love for this person." Or, "Dear Lord, I am encouraged to say that I am acting in a loving way toward my wife. I thank you for teaching me how to love her." Specifically and openly comparing your life with Scripture is a powerful way to draw the Bible through your will.

Visualize Scripture

The idea of Biblical Meditation through visualization is to take a passage of Scripture and make it come to life in your mind. It can be referred to as making a mental picture or movie of a biblical scene or concept. For thousands of years all societies have declared the power of the mind to shape behavior and achievement. There are at least two kinds of Scripture to visualize: narrative and didactic. **Narrative visualization** is where one sees a biblical story actually taking place. Smelling the smells; hearing the sounds around the event; touching the equipment or clothing of the individuals in the story. In narrative meditation there needs to be focused attention on the biblical detail and an educated imagination to fill out the narrative story line.

The second type of visualization is **didactic visualization**. This is where one pictures the truth of Scripture being lived out in present reality. When this is applied to doctrinal aspects of Scripture, the doctrinal truths are pictured. One might recognize the unseen hand of God moving on, in, and through the men who penned the Scripture to keep it error free and accurate. When this is applied to a practical principle for living, the principle is viewed as being lived out in life, such as being gentle in response to a sarcastic remark as in Proverbs 15:1. The key idea here is to actually picture oneself living out a scriptural concept. What has to be done to get in a position to live this biblical idea? If you can't see yourself doing a righteous idea in your mind, you will never do it. You have to see it before you will do it.

One of the clearest examples of this type of meditation is in Colossians 3:1-14. The apostle orders Christians to "set their minds on the things above;" "Put to death your earthly members: fornication, impurity, etc;" "Put on a heart of compassion, kindness, humility…" Each of these commands is a mental exercise designed to cause you to "see" what is not your present experience. We are to see ourselves enjoying the wonders of heaven, intimacy with God, the qualities of Christ, entering into the heavenly economy, etc. We are to picture ourselves as unresponsive and unaffected by those temptations that are the most powerful in our lives. We are to make a mental movie of the qualities of Christ being our normal lifestyle. Mental movie-making of biblical ideas is God's way of renewing our minds.

Personalize Scripture

Personalizing Scripture can bring the power of an individual Scripture directly into your emotions. This technique is accomplished by inserting your name or a personal pronoun into a verse when saying it. One of the reasons that the Psalms are such a popular section of the Scripture is that in many cases they are already personalized. Years ago I was counseling a woman who was really having a hard time staying in her marriage. She wanted to end her marriage and pursue her selfish desires. I asked her to pray and ask God what she should do. She began praying and God began to bring back into her mind the Scriptural directions for wives in Ephesians 5 with her name woven through the commands. This was immensely powerful. "God spoke to me," she said. "He spoke to me and I will never forget it." This time of prayerful meditation was a turning point in her life. She went back home and threw herself into her marriage with new hope and determination. Her marriage improved dramatically because God had spoken through Scripture as it was being personalized to her.

Record Insights

Usually during the time when you are using the other methods of biblical meditation you will become aware of ancillary questions, insights, connections, or bits of wisdom that are in some ways connected to the Scripture but may not be the main points of the passage. These are called insights. It is as though God begins to open the Scriptures to you and the levels of wisdom contained within it. Christians have usually found that if they write down insights as they are meditating, then they receive more of these insights. It is almost like saying to God, "I'm paying attention." Sometimes this is called spiritual journaling. A meditation journal is a helpful way of recording your reactions, thoughts, insights, and promptings during meditation.

Pray Scripture

This technique is to turn the actual phrases of Scripture into prayers. It is very educational to pray God's desires back to Him.

As your mind seeks ways to turn various passages into requests you will uncover new angles and depth of understanding on the will of God. In every passage there are many different ways to turn the truths into prayer requests. This type of prayer resembles the Apostle Paul's prayers in Ephesians 1:18-21 and 3:14-21. Asking for scriptural realities is often the best kind of praying for it keeps us from asking from a limited materialistic perspective. When we verbalize what God wants us to desire, we see the stark contrast between God's desires for us and our own fleshly desires.

Harmonize

There are at least two ways to meditate on Scripture through song. One is to sing the actual words of Scripture and adjust the tune to work with the unaltered words of the biblical text. The second method for meditating on Scripture through song is to take the truths, ideas, or concepts of the Scripture and sing those. This is a little easier and more free-flowing. When singing the Scripture it does not matter if it is great music, just that you are expressing the truths, feelings, and desires of Scripture. You will laugh, smile, ponder, and recommit to the Lord as you sing the words or concepts of Scripture. It is really an enjoyable process, but it takes a little courage to get started.

Open the Bible, pick a tune you know, and begin singing the words of Scripture to the tune. Another way to harmonize the Scripture is to look at a passage or a Christian doctrine and write down three or four truths. Start making up a song about those truths. The tune and the words are changeable as long as they accurately reflect the truth of Scripture. Many of our great hymns and gospel songs have come from just such meditations. The writers were not trying to write great hymns but to express their heart and soul regarding the truths of God. *Amazing Grace* by John Newton, *Amazing Love* by Charles Wesley, and various versions of the Apostles Creed that have been set to music are all examples of this type of meditation.

What are the results of Biblical Meditation?

God makes some amazing promises in the Scripture regarding biblical meditation. In Joshua 1:8 and Psalm 1:1-3, God promises believers if they meditate on His law they will be prosperous and successful. The mind filled with biblical principles and laws will avoid many of the hidden reefs that sink other people's lives. When a Christian purposefully fills their mind with Scripture, then the God of peace will move in and reassure that person that He is still in charge and He has a way through every storm (Colossians 3:16). In Psalm 119:97-100, God promises believers that they will gain wisdom beyond their years if they meditate upon biblical concepts.

When Are the Best Times to Meditate?

God has specifically suggested particular times to ruminate on Scripture (Deuteronomy 6:6-9; Psalm 1:1-3; 4:4; 63:6). **First,** the Scripture says to meditate when we sit in our homes. This means that one must turn off the TV at times. Many business travelers would lessen the temptations of travel and increase intimacy with God by turning off the television when they travel. **Second,** the Scripture suggests that people should get into the habit of reorienting their minds to Scripture as they are going from place to place. This is a time to pre-plan the next appointment using biblical concepts and qualities. A **third** time to meditate on Scripture is right before going to sleep. As people focus their minds on the concepts, qualities, and words of Scripture right before they drift off to sleep, it allows their subconscious mind to embrace these concepts. A **fourth** time to meditate each day is when the day begins. Many Christians set aside time each morning to spend extended time with God through

Biblical meditation. A **fifth** time for meditation is the night watches. These are times in the middle of the night spent with God and His word.

The Disciplines of Repetition: Conclusion

Memorization and meditation are not the only disciplines of repetition, but they have for centuries formed two of the more crucial practices that develop the spiritual Christian. It is not enough merely to understand these practices; one must actually do them on a regular basis to impact the depths of the soul. The goal of memorization and meditation is to give God the Holy Spirit an ever-increasing supply of language and concepts to use when communicating with us.

APPENDIX #3 BLANK WORKSHEETS

Please feel free to make copies of the blank worksheets. Both the Meditation work sheets and the Wisdom Search work sheets are yours to use. Many have found that keeping a small three-ring binder with these blank sheets in them is very helpful. I have put blank copies of these two worksheets on the next few pages. It is very rewarding to look back on the ways that God has led you in the past. These insights become a powerful guide and testimony to the work of the Lord in your life.

	Date: _____
Scripture	_____
Slow Repetition	_____
Memorization	_____
Study	_____
Singing	_____
Confessing	_____
Praying	_____
Envisioning	_____
Personalize	_____
Journal Insights	_____
Diagramming/ Analogy	_____
Personal Translation	_____

Appendix #3 Blank Worksheets

	Date: _____
Scripture	_____
Slow Repetition	_____
Memorization	_____
Study	_____
Singing	_____
Confessing	_____
Praying	_____
Envisioning	_____
Personalize	_____
Journal Insights	_____
Diagramming/ Analogy	_____
Personal Translation	_____

APPENDIX #4
HOW TO USE THIS BOOK

This book was written so that men and women would begin doing real Biblical Meditation. Therefore the projects and methods must be attempted in order to gain the full value of the book. There is little or no value in knowing that these work but not using them.

Personal Study

This book can be a personal study. If you are working through this book alone, then take each chapter and do the suggested exercise or wisdom search. Mark any exercises that are especially helpful so you will know for future reference. Some exercises need to be practiced for a week before their effectiveness is shown. If you find one exercise that is not helpful, then simply move on to the next exercise. Do not be in hurry to get through the book. Let the power of the Biblical Meditation get through you. If you find that one exercise is particularly helpful, then stay with that one exercise for a month or longer. In fact, that effective method may become the backbone of your whole devotional life. It is more important that you discover how to fill your mind with God's Word than that you finish the book in a certain time frame. This book may take you a year or longer to go through. Keep doing at least one new exercise per week until you have gone through the material at least once. You should be in a different place at the end of that cycle. You may then want to get into a group study in which you go through the material with others.

Mentor-Directed Study

This book can be done as a mentor-directed study. This is where a well respected, godly leader takes you through this material and evaluates your progress. Each week or month the mentor will assign chapters and exercises. The next time you gather together, give significant amounts of time to describing what happened when you tried Biblical Meditation. If they were not done or were not done well then the same exercises should be repeated. In my opinion the mentor-directed study is the most powerful and effective way of deploying this type of soul stretching material. One of the most effective ways I have seen a mentor-directed study get started is for the person with the desire for a mentor to ask a person that they highly respect to mentor them over this material. The mentor is asked if they would be willing to meet with the individual or small group and walk them through the material.

A second way that a mentor-directed study can be initiated is by the mentor. He/she can pray and ask the Lord to direct them to those who might be ready for a deeper spiritual growth study like this one. Either by phone or in person, ask people whom God has put on your heart if they would be interested in growing deeper through a weekly study of this type. If they say, yes, then sign them up and put them in a small group of people like themselves. If they say, no, then that is okay; they are just not ready.

Class, Groups, or Lecture series

This book can be covered as a Bible Study Class, a small group, an Adult Sunday School Class, a Men's or Women's Ministry Class. If there are less than six people in the class I would recommend that you adopt the mentor format rather than the class style. But if there are seven or more, then the lecture style can work quiet well. The best class format divides an hour and a half into three approximately equal segments of about thirty minutes. Start with prayer and about twenty to thirty minutes of sharing in small groups of three or four people of the same gender about how the exercises went from the last week. If there is wide spread misunderstanding on the exercises that were taught the last time, then they should be explained again. Then there should be a twenty-to-thirty minute lecture on the next set of exercises. Remember that the goal is not to have people impressed with the teacher. The goal is to have a deep relationship with Jesus. That will only take place if they are actually doing the exercises. Finally in a class or study, twenty to thirty minutes should be set aside for actually doing the exercise in class. Have the people in the class actually try out the exercises. Then have the class commit to doing the exercises during the week.

Remember the goal is demonstrated skill in filling one's mind with Scripture. If an exercise needs to be repeated, then repeat it. When the class is over, take a few weeks or a month off and then start teaching the class again. If your church is larger, start a new class every month or two. There does not need to be large attendance for this class. In fact, it is almost better if the class is limited to less than twelve at a time.

Activity or Spiritual Exercise Class

Finding the motivation to do biblical exercises on your own is difficult. For this reason, some individuals and churches have found that classes in which a leader guides people through the exercises is very helpful. This is like an exercise class at a gym. Everyone could exercise at home, but they go to the gym and take a step class or Pilates class or one of a hundred other classes that will help them increase the amount of physical exercise in their life. These spiritual exercise classes are not designed to teach you something new but instead to help you regularly practice something you already know is good. This was the original idea behind prayer meetings in church. It was a regular time each week that would encourage people to pray longer. In this case a Biblical Meditation class would move you through one to three different Biblical Meditation exercises. The leader would determine the exercises and the verses that would be meditated upon. If a person came to class they would have done something very good for their soul.

OTHER MATERIALS BY GIL STIEGLITZ

BOOKS
Becoming a Godly Husband
Becoming a Godly Wife (with Dana Stieglitz)
Going Deep In Prayer: 40 Days of In-Depth Prayer
Leading a Thriving Ministry: 10 Indispensable Leadership Skills
Marital Intelligence: A Foolproof Guide for Saving and Strengthening Marriage
Mission Possible: Winning the Battle over Temptation
Spiritual Disciplines of a C.H.R.I.S.T.I.A.N.: Intensive Training in Christian Spirituality
Touching the Face of God: 40 Days of Adoring God

VIDEOS
Growing a Healthy and Vibrant Church
Marital Intelligence: There are Only Five Problems in Marriage

AUDIO
The Ten Commandments
God's Principles for Handling Money
Becoming a Godly Parent

If you would be interested in having Dr. Gil Stieglitz speak to your group, you can contact him through the web site

www.ptlb.com

www.ingramcontent.com/pod-product-compliance
Lightning Source LLC
LaVergne TN
LVHW040116080426
835507LV00039B/383